REVIVAL

And the Apostolic Church in the Monmouthshire Valleys

Jason Pennington

REVIVAL and the Apostolic Church in the Monmouthshire Valleys by Jason Pennington

First Published in Great Britain in 2016

FAITHBUILDERS PUBLISHING www.biblestudiesonline.org.uk

An Imprint of Apostolos Publishing Ltd,

3rd Floor, 207 Regent Street,

London W1B 3HH

www.apostolos-publishing.com

British Library Cataloguing-in-Publication Data

A catalogue record for this book is available from the British Library

ISBN: 978-1-910942-60-4

Cover Design by Blitz Media, Pontypool, Torfaen, UK

First printed in Great Britain

Foreword

January 2016 marks the 100th anniversary of the Apostolic Church in the UK. In commemoration of the centenary, this book is being presented in order to provide a brief history of the work of the Apostolic Church in the Monmouthshire Valleys. In this history you will read about the people, the events, and the places that gave rise to the Apostolic Church in the Monmouthshire Valleys and those who have continued its distinctive testimony. Today the district is referred to as the North Gwent district, covering churches in the Counties of Monmouthshire and Blaenau Gwent. With other church assemblies, once included in the Monmouthshire Valleys Area (Beaufort Area), now referred to as the Newport district.

As the older generations pass away, the memories of the events that took place fade. Gratitude must be given to those in previous generations, who have taken the trouble to make notes and records of our local history. Thanks are also due to the older members of the congregations who have contributed photographs, memories, and invaluable information towards the compiling of this book. Those who can still remember something of the beginnings of the work of the Apostolic church in the Monmouthshire Valleys have been invaluable.

Included in this book are the written testimonies and the life stories of a number of individuals who were involved in the beginning of Apostolic churches in the Monmouthshire Valleys.

Contents

Introduction

This book examines the emergence of the Apostolic Church in Monmouthshire at the turn of the nineteenth/twentieth century. At that time, Monmouthshire was bordered by the counties of Brecon and Glamorgan in Wales and the counties of Hereford and Gloucester in England, covering an area from Abergavenny in the North to the Severn Estuary in the South and from Monmouth and Chepstow in the East to Tredegar and Newport in the West.

With its origins in the Welsh Revival of 1904, the Apostolic Church has been a denomination that was both inspired and led by God's Holy Spirit. The same must be said of the beginnings and growth of the Apostolic Church in the Monmouthshire Valleys.

It is remarkable how God has moved amongst the mining and steel making communities of the Monmouthshire valleys to call out a people and a church for himself. The people God has called have been no less remarkable, men and women of exceptional character and some, real 'diamonds in the rough'.

The postmodern, western society of the late twentieth and early twenty-first century has seen the emergence of the consumer driven mind-set and with it the appearance of 'consumer' or 'entertainment' driven church. The late author Roy Hession, having himself experienced revival in the 1940s, makes the following observation of Western Christianity:

> There tends to be today an emphasis on the seeking of inner spiritual experiences. While so many Christians are content to live at a very low level, it is good that some do become concerned about their Christian lives, and it is right that

they should. However, the concern arises not so much from a hunger for God, but from a longing to find an inner experience of happiness, joy, and power, and we find ourselves looking for "it", rather than God Himself. Both these ends fall utterly short of the great end that God has designed for man, that of glorifying Him and enjoying Him forever. They fail to satisfy God's heart and they fail to satisfy ours.[1]

Whilst there are many admirable mission programs, many large churches, and many social gospel endeavours around the UK, church attendance is generally in decline. Statistics suggest that in 2015 church membership accounts for just 11% of the British population by comparison to 33% in 1900.[2] We have only to look at the national statistics on crime and consumer spending to see morality is slipping from the grasp of our nation and that our society is increasingly self-seeking and entertainment driven.

There is a great need for a spiritual revival. Not a revival for inner experiences, not a revival to make denominational celebrities, nor a revival to build spiritual dynasties, but a revival that will turn the hearts of men and women back to God. A revival that will once again turn Christian thinking away from the success-driven mentality of post modernism and back to the life-surrendered, servant mentality of Christ.

One of the great hallmarks of the early Apostolic pioneers was their openness to prophetic revelation for help and direction. Particularly

---

[1] Roy Hession, *We Would See Jesus* (Wendover: Rickfords 1958; repr. 2008), 4.
[2] *British Religion in Numbers* <http://www.brin.ac.uk/2011/uk-church-statistics-2005-15>.

through the channel of the prophet, decisions were shaped by the utterance of a 'word from God'. Though some Pentecostals were opposed to such practices, the benefit of prophetic direction was evidenced in the way God was confirming his prophetic word, blessing and building the work of the Apostolic Church.

As we look at the remarkable things that God accomplished, through the lives of men and women who were changed by revival outpourings and Pentecostal awakenings, it is also important to remember the sacrificial giving that marked a poor generation as one of the most generous. It becomes clear that men and women encountered God in a powerful way and as a result achieved much. I see the Apostolic Church in the UK and in other nations as a lasting legacy of such dedicated workers. If we desire to see a spiritual awakening, with lives saved and changed by the power of God, then we need another revival in the modern day, and our prayer must surely be; God revive us!

In the early days of rising Pentecostalism, the motor car was a rare commodity, the majority of people having to walk or use public transport to travel any distance. Mostly people walked, to work, to the public house, the shops, to school, and to their chapel. Times were hard, money was short, and walking was free. It was not uncommon for people to walk five or ten miles, or even further. With this in mind, it is remarkable how the early work of the Pentecostal churches spread.

People often travelling by whatever means available in order to hold open air meetings, church services, evangelistic events and church planting. Others relocated, moving home from one town to another. With God at their side, no task was too big, no distance too far!

The early pioneers must be credited with accomplishing so much with so little resources. Come rain, snow, or shine, nothing discouraged the early believers of the Pentecostal movement in the Monmouthshire valleys from getting to meetings and worshiping the Lord. Often managing with just enough to feed their families, and yet trusting God they gave sacrificially. These were Pentecostal believers who raised enough money to build church buildings, salary pastors, and sponsor missionaries.

Today, with the use of a car available to most households, there is far less need for smaller local churches. Small communities, once isolated by geography and limited transport, are now far less isolated. As a result of this and the changing economic and social factors affecting the South Wales valleys, many of the smaller churches have been closed in recent years and, or amalgamated with neighbouring ones. Today the Apostolic Church in North Gwent worships in just two locations, one in Abergavenny and the other in Ebbw Vale. Similarly, in the Newport district, the Apostolic church worships in Pontllanfraith and Newport. These churches represent the present work of the Apostolic Church in what was once known as the Monmouthshire valleys.

Social Setting

At the turn of the twentieth century the main employment in the Monmouthshire valleys was to be found working in the coal, iron, or steel industries. Life was hard, work was dangerous, and if you couldn't work there was no unemployment benefits so people had to rely on handouts or what little savings you might have had. At that time death and disability were a common occurrence of working life. There was no National Health Service therefore health care was also hit and miss, often dependent on whether your employment included insurance for health care or if the individual could afford medical treatment.

Domestic life was little better, with high infant mortality and women suffering from the poor social conditions of the day. Karen Lowe in her book 'Carriers of the Fire'[3] remarks how death and debilitation through frequent child birth and domestic labour affected housewives of the time. Household injuries being just as common place as those in the workplace. Many young women had to leave home to go into domestic service. For others it was work in one of the many local shops with long hours and often for little pay. The 1890s had seen considerable civil unrest, strikes, and disputes over low pay and unfair treatment.

Complaints, particularly against the coal mine owners and management, had resulted in walk outs and strike action, leading to a rise in the strength of trade unions in the area. However, by the early part of the nineteen-hundreds in the northern Monmouthshire valleys there was growth and modernisation as local industry developed. Modern deep pits such as those at Waunlwyd and Cwm would take over production as older mines neared their end.[4] New steel plant including the latest blast furnace at Victoria and new machinery replacing the old Bessemer steel plant brought increased productivity and further growth to the area. This in turn caused a rapid increase in the population over the first ten years of the

---

[3] Karen Lowe, *Carriers of the Fire, The Women of the Welsh Revival 1904/05* (Llanelli: Shedhead Productions, 2004), 8–11.
[4] Cwm Community Care <http://www.cwmcommunitycare.org.uk/waunlwyd-victoria-collierie/4558107657>.

twentieth century. The town of Ebbw Vale in particular increased from a population of 21,000 to 31,000 from 1901–1914 leading to considerable expansion and rebuilding in the town.[5] The scene was one of constant industrial activity with all its steam, smoke, and grime. Politically there were changes as Trade Unions were rising to increasing strength and Socialism had gained a strong foot hold in the industrial heartland of the South Wales valleys. As yet women had no vote, and were not permitted to stand for election, but the suffrage movement was increasingly active in the cause for women's rights. Votes and 'equal rights' for women in the UK would not be completely introduced until 1928.[6]

Church Life

Although at times there were divisions between conformist and non-conformist church groups, churches were generally well established and well attended. In the valleys, people were loyal to 'their' chapel, and although many had fallen into irregular attendance, they would still consider the church or chapel historically attended by their family as being 'theirs'. Attendance had been affected, the publication of Charles Darwin's 'Origin of Species' in 1859, the rise of Liberalism and the "Higher Criticism" method of study had each led to reduced confidence in the church and particularly the Bible.[7] For many, the church was becoming less relevant in everyday life; chapels were becoming places for births,

---

[5] Arthur Gray-Jones, *A History of Ebbw Vale* (Rogerstone: Gwent County Council 1970; 2nd Ed. 1992), 210–211.

[6] <http://www.parliament.uk/about/living-heritage/transformingsociety>.

[7] <http://www.nhm.ac.uk/galleries/galleries-home/treasures/specimens/darwin-origins/>.

deaths and marriages, as men and women looked to science to answer their problems. Reports of low attendance at Sunday services, complaints of religious indifference, and a distinct falling away in church membership were common at the turn of the twentieth century.[8] In spite of this many church groups and movements continued their social missions and evangelistic programs. The Holiness movement, which had arisen from the Methodist church in America in the 1800s was of considerable influence, finding expression amongst other places at the Keswick conventions in the UK and promoting spiritual renewal.[9] The Keswick in Wales Conferences held at Llandrindod Wells were particularly influential in South Wales. Another group was William Booth's Salvation Army who were continually engaged in social mission and evangelising the masses. Independent and Congregational churches also sought to address the social issues that were prevalent at the turn of the century. The world-wide movement of prayer circles, had started in the early 1890s and by the end of the decade a number of revival prayer groups or circles had been set up specifically to pray for revival in Wales.[10]

---

[8] Eifion Evans, *The Welsh Revival of 1904* (London: Evangelical Press, 1969; 2nd Ed. 1974), 44–45.
[9] David Allen, *The Unfailing Stream, A Charismatic Church History in Outline* (Tonbridge, Sovereign World, 1994), 72–74.
[10] John Hayward, *Timeline of the Background to 1904-5 Welsh Revival* (2004) <http://www.churchmodel.org.uk/Timelineback04.pdf>, 3

Revival

Wales has been called the 'land of revival'. Eifion Evans in his book 'Revival Comes to Wales' comments that between 1762 and 1862 there were at least fifteen outstanding revivals in Wales. From North to South, East to West, Wales has experienced times of marked spiritual awakening. Whole communities had been affected for the better by the visiting of God's presence upon them. Each 'outpouring' was distinct in character but identical in the results of souls saved, increased church attendance, and general moral improvement.[11]

Monmouthshire was no exception. The Congregational churches in that locality alone estimated at least two thousand people had been added between 1859 and 1860. In particular the Congregational Church at Beaufort, Ebbw Vale, benefited from a special assembly of Congregational churches organised by minister T. Rees in June 1859. Later that year non-conformist churches in Ebbw Vale sent a group to Llangeitho in order to press revivalist David Morgan to visit Monmouthshire. Although at first he declined, after a rousing appeal, the group prevailed.[12] Again in 1899 'Church Revival at Beaufort' was the title of an article in the Western Mail reporting that at St. Andrews Parish Church, Beaufort Hill, eighty-two adults and infants were baptised over that Easter Sunday, a good number being adults.[13] Although this was in stark contrast to the general spiritual condition prevalent at the time. There were other

---

[11] Eifion Evans, *Revival Comes to Wales, The Story of the 1859 Revival in Wales* (Bridgend, Evangelical Press of Wales 1959 3rd Ed. 1986), 10.

[12] Evans, *Revival Comes to Wales*, 87–88

[13] *The Western Mail* 7th April 1899. <http://newspapers.library.wales/>.

evangelistic efforts, in 1901 the British Free Church Council were calling for a concerted effort to hold united evangelical missions across the country. Also the Forward Movement were working tirelessly in the industrial areas of South Wales.[14]

In 1904, Wales was again gripped with spiritual 'revival' as countless men and women came to faith, filled with a deep desire to know Jesus Christ.[15] Referring to this revival and the marked spiritual intensity of conviction that it brought, D. P. Williams writes:

> When the Spirit of God was so tremendously poured out in 1904, prayer was heard like the sound of cannon in the day of battle. The enemies of the King fell in their thousands, mown down like grass in chapels, homes, streets, stations and trains, and even down in the bowels of the earth, for Heaven had come down at the cry of them that had humbled themselves in the hour of visitation.[16]

Churches and chapels were packed to hear Mr. Evan Roberts, the principle figure of the Welsh Revival, speak under the influence of the Holy Spirit. God was using others, men and women who were also at work in the revival, as it spread across South Wales.[17]

---

[14] Evans, *The Welsh Revival of 1904*, Chapter 2

[15] S. B. Shaw, *The Great Revival in Wales* (Pensecola FL: Christian Life Books, 2002).

[16] D. P. Williams, *The Work of an Evangelist: his Calling, Qualifications and Equipment* (Llanelli: Apostolic Church, circa 1928).

[17] D. P. Williams, *The Prophetical Ministry (or the Voice Gifts) in the Church* (Llanelli: Apostolic Church, 1931).

In North Monmouthshire, Sam Jenkins and Sydney Evans visited Ebbw Vale in January 1905.[18] The event was covered by articles in a number of newspapers including the *Evening Express* and the *Cardiff Times*. In the *Cardiff Times and South Wales Weekly* on Saturday 21st of January the following report on the revival meetings in Ebbw Vale was published:

MR SIDNEY EVANS AT EBBW VALE.

Crowded Meetings all Day.

The three days' mission at Ebbw Vale by Mr. Sidney Evans and party, under the auspices of the Ebbw Vale and District Free Church Council, was continued with unabated vigour on Monday. Providence Baptist Chapel was found far too small to accommodate the large congregation that assembled in the afternoon. The blinding snowstorm did not interfere in any way with the fervor of the people and an adjournment was made to Libanus Congregational Chapel close by, which supplied the necessary accommodation. Mr. Sidney Evans, the missioner, made an impressive address, and as the result of the usual test 45 converts were enrolled. Saron Congregational Chapel was the place set apart for the night meeting, and although one of the largest buildings in the town it was packed long before the appointed time. Prior to the arrival of the missioners the proceedings were led by Mr. T. M. Jeffreys, secretary of the Free Church Council, and the Rev. T. Tudor, pastor. The congregation was full of the Spirit. Song and prayer broke out from all parts of the

---

[18] *Evening Express* 17th January 1905. <http://newspapers.library.wales/>.

building. It was rumoured that the mission that was being conducted at Waunlwyd at the same time required assistance. One young man shouted out, I have never done anything for Christ, but will go to Waunlwyd and help. I have been a theatre goer, and will work for Christ in the future. Several others also volunteered. In reply to an invitation from the Rev. T. Tudor a score at least volunteered to keep away from the theatre and the public house. On the arrival of Mr. Sidney Evans and his fellow missioners the story of Pentecost was read by Mr. James, a student of Trefecca College. He invited silent prayer and told the congregation to remain silent until the Spirit told them to do otherwise. The prompting of the Spirit was at once manifest in outbursts of prayer and singing in all parts. Mr. Evans opened by saying that he had asked God to save people in that meeting. He would answer his prayer. Some people on the gallery were going to be saved that night. The Christian could not accept dirty money, he said. A gambler who had won £50 by a bet, upon being converted, refused to take it because it was "dirty money." Young people could not be damned by the Devil but by themselves. If they could not open their hearts themselves let God have a try. The missioner submitted the usual test, and the workers were soon busy among the numerous inquirers."[19]

The impact this revival had upon Christian life in South Wales and the South Wales Valleys cannot be underestimated. A report appearing in one South Wales newspaper listed the numbers and

---

[19] *Cardiff Times & South Wales Weekly* 21st January 1905.

locations of new converts. In Ebbw Vale 1720 souls were listed as having been converted, and many more besides in the surrounding towns and villages.[20] One writer described the way in which the revival spread as 'like a mighty prairie fire all over South Wales and Monmouthshire', estimating that in three months one hundred and seventy-five thousand souls were converted.[21]

One example of the impact the revival had on local communities, is recorded by the landlord of the Foresters Arms, Blaenau who is reported as blaming the revival for 'having contributed to the closure of his business.'[22] William Robins, a man saved during the 1904 revival, writes of his own change of heart, no longer drinking in public houses and making reparation for debts owed and items taken prior to his conversion.[23] Mr. Robins' testimony is typical of the change that was taking place in the lives of those affected by the revival as they were gripped by a new found sense of morality and spiritual passion. S. B. Shaw remarks that as far as drunkenness and revelry were concerned, the Christmas of 1904 was the most peaceful South Wales had ever known.[24]

In 1901, across the Atlantic Ocean in America, a group of students at Bethel Bible College in Topeka, Kansas experienced the Holy Spirit baptism for the first time. The college founder and teacher was Charles Fox Parham. Following this initial Pentecostal

---

[20] K. Adams & E. A. Jones, *Pictorial History of Revival: The Outbreak of the 1904 Welsh Awakening* (Farnham; CWR 2004).
[21] Price Davies, *The Beginning of the Pentecostal Movement in the Merthyr Borough* <www.dustandashes.com> c. 1960.
[22] *Weekly Mail* 18th March 1905. <http://newspapers.library.wales/>.
[23] See Appendix 1 Testimony of William Robbins.
[24] Shaw, *The Great Revival*, 58.

outpouring he began to preach the Pentecostal experience and establish Apostolic Faith churches. There were thousands of converts baptised in the Spirit and a number of churches established throughout Texas.[25] By 1906, The Apostolic Faith Church, Asuza Street, Los Angeles was the setting for Pentecostal revival. The minister there was Bishop William J. Seymour, an African American pastor, who had attended a ten-week training session on the baptism of the Holy Spirit at Parham's Bible College in Houston, Texas. The baptism of the Holy Spirit was in full evidence, fervent prayer was constant, as was 'singing in the Spirit'. With the circulation of their own newsletter, 'Apostolic Faith' and local newspaper coverage of events, news of the revival spread in all directions. There were many visitors to Asuza Street including T. B. Barratt, an Englishman living in Norway. Barratt an ordained minister was visiting America to raise funds for his Oslo City Mission. Upon reading an issue of Apostolic Faith, he received his baptism with the Holy Spirit whilst on his own in his hotel room in New York![26]

Barratt became a pivotal figure in the spread of European Pentecostal movement; he was particularly influential in Britain especially through his links to Rev. Alexander A. Boddy at Sunderland.

---

[25] Allen, *The Unfailing Stream,* 107–109.
[26] T. B. Barrat, *In the Days of the Latter Rain* (London: Elim Publishing Co. 1909 2nd Edition, 1928).

Sunderland

Alexander Boddy was an Anglican minister at All Saints Church, Monkwearmouth, Sunderland. He had visited Wales during the 1904–5 revival to hear Evan Roberts and had been deeply moved and impressed by the moving of the Holy Spirit in the gathering. Upon returning to Sunderland and with a desire to see revival, Boddy began to hold revival prayer meetings with a small group of his parishioners. News began to reach him, first of the Pentecostal revival in Asuza Street, and then of a Pentecostal revival that had broken out in Norway under the ministry of Pastor T. B. Barratt. Boddy visited Norway and invited Barratt to come and speak to the group at 'All Saints.' During September and October 1907 Pastor Barratt came and ministered in Sunderland. The result was that many received the baptism of the Holy Spirit with the evidence of speaking in tongues. Of note amongst those early visitors was a man by the name of Smith Wigglesworth. Later to become a world famous 'healing evangelist', Wigglesworth received his baptism in the Holy Spirit during a prayer meeting at All Saints Sunderland.[27] By April 1908 Boddy recorded that the number of those receiving the 'baptism' had reached seventy.[28]

There was much opposition to the new teaching emerging from Sunderland. Prominent church leaders such as Reader Harris, founder of the ironically named 'Pentecostal League of Prayer', F. B. Meyer, Campbell Morgan, and also prominent women such as Revivalist Jessie Penn Lewis of the Keswick Conventions and close

---

[27] Smith Wigglesworth <www.smithwigglesworth.com>.
[28] W. K. Kay, "Sunderland's Legacy in New Denominations," *JEPTA* 28(2) (2008), 183–199.

friend to Evan Roberts.[29] These and others had been strongly in favour of revival and advocates of the Holiness movement were increasingly opposed to speaking in tongues.[30]

Boddy began publishing Confidence in April 1908 this was a specifically Pentecostal newspaper which helped to promote the Pentecostal experience.[31] Led by God and in spite of the growing opposition, he committed to holding an annual 'Pentecostal Whitsuntide Convention' at Sunderland. An invitation was sent out and many came to this first convention in June 1908.

The conventions would continue until the outbreak of the First World War in 1914.[32] Tickets were produced for the event and although given freely, they were used to limit entrance only to those sympathetic to Pentecostalism and speaking in tongues.[33]

Of significant help to Alexander Boddy and very much a part of the Pentecostal work at Sunderland from the early stages was Cecil Polhill who had himself visited Asuza Street.[34] Polhill, himself a wealthy landowner, had spent twenty years as a missionary in China before returning to Britain and remained a member of the Council for the China Inland Mission until his death.[35]

---

[29] Jessie Penn-Lewis and Evan Roberts, *War on the Saints*. Unabridged Edition (Kent: Diasozo Trust, 1973; 9th ed. 1987).
[30] Allen, *The Unfailing Stream,* 120.
[31] *Confidence* Issue 1 <http://pentecostalarchives.org>.
[32] Donald Gee, *The Pentecostal Movement: A Short History and An Interpretation for British Readers* (Ebook, Read Books Ltd, 2013), 42.
[33] *Confidence* Issue 1, 2.
[34] Allen, *The Unfailing Stream,* 119.
[35] Gee, *The Pentecostal Movement,* 52–56.

Waunlwyd

Waunlwyd Village 1910, Colliery in foreground. Courtesy of Ebbw Vale Museum.
Tabernacle Church is left of centre near the chimney stack.

Following the 1904–05 revival and the meetings that had taken place in Ebbw Vale, the work in Waunlwyd continued. A small mining village near Ebbw Vale in the Monmouthshire Valleys, Waunlwyd was growing as a result of the new deep pit colliery that had opened there.[36] The newly built Tabernacle, an English-language Congregational chapel, was the setting for the next stage of Pentecostal development in the Monmouthshire Valleys.

Rev. Thomas Madog Jeffreys was a member of the local Free Church Council, which had arranged the visit of revivalist Sydney Evans and

---

[36] Gray-Jones, *A History of Ebbw Vale*, 187-190.

his associates to Ebbw Vale. Jeffreys was ordained as minister of the new Tabernacle Congregational Church, Waunlwyd in June 1906, following in the footsteps of his father and grandfather, both of whom had been Congregational ministers. He had given up a promising and successful career as Headmaster at a school in Aberystwyth in order to enter the ministry himself.[37]

During this period William Robins joined the Tabernacle. Robins having returned from Pontymoile to work at the Waunllwyd colliery. His own written account is of great help in detailing the events that followed. At first there appears to have been a measure of reservation from some of the deacons towards Mr. Robins as he had been baptised by immersion in water, a practice not held by Congregationalists. There was clearly a deep spiritual desire amongst a core of believers led by Rev. Jeffreys at the Tabernacle. Robins describes the church as having 'the Revival Spirit' still in evidence.

Rev. Jeffreys would later write:

> ever since the Welsh Revival, our little church has nursed the Fire; our meetings have been kept, 'open, open-air work and tract distribution, together with cottage prayer meetings and the relieving of the sick and necessitous, have been the means of great blessing to a staunch little band of Overcomers'.[38]

---

[37] *The Carmarthen Weekly Reporter* 29th June 1906 <http://newspapers.library.wales/>
[38] *Confidence* Issue 1, 13–14.

Mr and Mrs Robins in later life outside Waunlwyd Apostolic Church

In September 1906 during a Monday night prayer meeting, with eight or nine present including Rev. Jeffries and Mr. Robins, the Holy Spirit descended upon the group. Mr. Robins, overcome by an unusual sensation, told his friend 'I shall have to go out, I am dying to laugh' at which point his friend began to laugh and now both could not stop laughing.

Amongst others, Jeffreys worked closely in the local Free Church Council with Rev. T. Tudor, the minister of Saron Congregational Church, Ebbw Vale. Interestingly, Rev Jeffreys' grandfather had been the minister of Saron 40 years earlier. Towards the end of 1906 the Ebbw Vale Free Church Council organised a twelve-day mission.[39]

Rev. W. S. Jones, Llwynypia was the guest speaker, himself an anointed revivalist. During the mission, meetings were distributed around the locality, six days for Ebbw Vale, three days for Beaufort and three days for Waunlwyd and Victoria. The meetings were a tremendous success, T. M. Jeffreys now finding himself overcome with laughter and many prostrate under the power of the Holy Spirit. Given the success of the mission, another was organised, this time by the free churches at 'the bottom end' of Ebbw Vale, Waunlwyd and Victoria.

It was decided that given the experience of the last mission W. S. Jones should be booked again and the mission was arranged for November 1907.

The week before these meetings were due to begin, Rev. Jeffreys received a telegram from W. S. Jones stating that he had been taken ill and was unable to come. With such little time to make new arrangements the decision was taken to ask W. S. Jones to find a suitable replacement [Appendix 1]. God was at work in a miraculous way, organising his program for the coming event.

Pastor A. Moncur Niblock of Aston Birmingham had received a word from God that he was to travel to Wales.[40] He had already packed his case and was prayerfully waiting for the next direction from God when a telegram from W. S. Jones arrived asking him to

---

[39] *The Carmarthen Weekly Reporter* 29th June 1906. <http://newspapers.library. wales/>
[40] *Confidence* Issue 1, 13.

be his replacement at the Ebbw Vale meetings, this was his call to go! The question that was now much in the thoughts of the group from Waunlwyd was; could they expect the experience according to Acts chapter two, that is a definite baptism with the Holy Spirit? This question was put to Pastor Niblock during the mission and his response was "Yes, of course." Although seeking, as yet, Pastor Niblock had not received the baptism of the Holy Spirit. Again the mission was deemed a tremendous success, some wanting to continue the meetings, however it was decided to draw the mission to a close. The small group of believers at the Tabernacle decided to continue on their own. They began holding tarry meetings every night seeking this experience of Pentecost and these continued right up to the Christmas. William Robbins writes "It is impossible for me to describe the awe of the presence of God in those meetings."[41]

In his first letter to the 'Confidence' Pentecostal newsletter,[42] Jeffreys writes that the tarrying or waiting meetings began on 1st December 1907 and that he had received prophecy concerning 'when the heavens would open' (quoting Daniel 9:23).

> At the beginning of thy supplications the commandment came forth, and I am come to shew thee, for thou art greatly beloved: therefore understand the matter and consider the vision. (KJV)

And also Daniel 10 v.13:

> But the prince of the kingdom of Persia withstood me one and twenty days: but lo, Michael, one of the chief princes,

---

[41] Appendix 1 Testimony of William Robbins.
[42] *Confidence* Issue 1, 14.

came to help me; and I remained there with the kings of
Persia. (KJV)

As the church was in use for their annual Christmas events, on
December 22nd the tarry meeting moved to the home of T. M.
Jeffreys. One of the members present was John Jones, who had
overcome much opposition from his wife in order to be there (his
wife had hidden all his shoes in the hope of stopping him from
going to the tarry meeting).

However, he found an old pair of 'slaps' (similar to flip-flops) under
the stairs and walked to the meeting in them, in the middle of
winter! Sure enough the Spirit fell in that meeting, John Jones was
filled with the Holy Spirit and began to speak in other tongues.
Things did not stop there, the group met again the following day as
the outpouring continued. Jeffreys describes what followed
declaring, 'glorious experiences, too many to attempt to describe,
have been ours.' Seven in all, including Rev. Jeffreys received the
Pentecostal baptism with the sign of tongues during those meetings.
He later writes 'The definite seeking for Baptismal Fullness began
as a result of a mission conducted by Pastor Niblock, of Aston, in
November last.'[43]

There was more opposition, some declaring that they had gone mad
and the persecution intensified. Of those in opposition to these
Pentecostal manifestations, many tried to find biblical evidence
against such practices. One local minister is quoted as having
preached a sermon on the text, tongues shall cease.[44]

---

[43] *Confidence* Issue 1, 13–14.
[44] Appendix 1 Testimony of William Robbins.

Despite the prejudice and opposition, things continued and now others searching for a 'second blessing' or Pentecostal experience began to come from everywhere in the surrounding areas. The leader of the Salvation Army Corp at Cwm visited Jeffreys and whilst Jeffreys prayed, he was baptised in the Holy Spirit.[45] Not long after the mission, Pastor Niblock visited All Saints, Sunderland where he received his Holy Spirit baptism and began 'speaking in tongues'. He now returned to Waunlwyd accompanied by American A. H. Post of Los Angeles.[46] Pastor A. H. Post was a church leader who was now on his way to become a missionary in Colombo, Ceylon (now Sri Lanka). He had received his Spirit baptism in Los Angeles in 1906 and had been involved in prayer meetings held for church leaders by W. J. Seymor at Asuza Street.[47] Both Pastors Niblock and Post brought much encouragement to the group, stirring them to continue actively seeking for the baptism with the Holy Spirit. During Easter 1908 Pastors Niblock and Post were at the Tabernacle, Waunlwyd, providing ministry and encouragement.[48] Visitors came to the convention at Waunlwyd from Abertillery approximately 5½ miles distance, Maesycwmmer 12 miles; Dowlais 10 miles and Merthyr approximately 14 miles. Amongst those visiting, four young men had come over the mountain from

---

[45] *Confidence* Issue 2 May 1908, 10 <http://pentecostalarchives.org>.

[46] *The Apostolic Faith* Volume 2 No.13 (May, 1908) <www.apostolicfaith.org/Library/Index/AzusaPapers.aspx>.

[47] H. D. Hunter and C. M. Robeck Jnr, *The Asuza Street Revival and Its Legacy* (Eugene, Oregon, Wipf and Stock 2006, 2nd Ed 2009).

[48] Davies, *The Beginning of the Pentecostal Movement.*

Dowlais, all four were baptised in the Spirit and carried the fire back with them![49]

Donald Gee, himself a pioneer of the Assemblies of God churches in Britain, describes how this Pentecostal work then spread from Dowlais to Aberamman.[50] Amongst the four was Price Davies, a man who had been saved at Mountain Ash under the ministry of Evan Roberts during the 1904 revival. Price Davies and T. M. Jeffreys appear to have developed a close relationship, Jeffreys later presiding at his wedding.[51]

Davies would later have considerable influence in the establishment of the Assemblies of God churches in the region, including at Crosskeys and Newbridge.[52] He, with others, would regularly visit the home of George and Stephen Jeffreys (no relation to T. M. Jeffreys) both of whom would become world famous. Price Davies had the privilege of baptising Stephen and at a later time George in water.[53] Stephen Jeffreys would go on to become a renowned evangelist working independently with a number of churches and groups, particularly the Assemblies of God. His brother, George Jeffreys, would be the key figure in establishing the Elim Pentecostal churches.[54]

One remarkable occurrence was that another group at an Easter convention in Gorseinon near Swansea were at that same time

[49] *Confidence* Issue 2, 10.
[50] Gee, *The Pentecostal Movement*, 71.
[51] Davies, *The Beginning of the Pentecostal Movement*.
[52] Chris Palmer, *The Emergence of Pentecostalism in Wales* (London: Apostolos, 2016), 138–139.
[53] Davies, *The Beginning of the Pentecostal Movement*.
[54] Gee, *The Pentecostal Movement*, 41.

having an identical experience. The Holy Spirit also being poured out there. A prophecy was given during those meetings telling of the group in Waunlwyd and God's outpouring there.[55]

Amongst those visiting Swansea who received the baptism with the Holy Spirit and speaking in tongues was a Pastor Hodges from Hereford.[56] Hodges received his Spirit baptism whilst praying with the Pentecostal people he was staying with in Lougher.[57]

Robins in his testimony[58] and Pastor Jeffreys commenting at Sunderland[59] both recount the remarkable healing miracles that were taking place at Waunlwyd. T. M. Jeffreys also commented on news of a new outpouring in a neighbouring village with thirteen having received the baptism with the 'sign of tongues'.[60] The events that had taken place at Waunlwyd were now being carried to neighbouring villages. This new Pentecostal experience was beginning to spread. A revival was taking place as others were catching the fire!

---

[55] Gee, *The Pentecostal Movement*, 41.
[56] Davies, *The Beginning of the Pentecostal Movement.*
[57] Apostolic Church, *Souvenir.*
[58] Appendix 1 Testimony of William Robbins.
[59] *Confidence* Issue 2, 10.
[60] *Confidence* Issue 1, 13–14.

The Sunderland Connection

The Rev. Alexander Boddy organised a Pentecostal Convention at All Saints Church Sunderland over the Whitsun period in 1908. In 'Confidence,' Boddy refers to an advert that had been placed in a Cardiff newspaper, for cheap excursions to Sunderland for the convention.[61] Articles printed in the first few publications of Confidence provide evidence of the geographical spread of those writing to Boddy.[62] T. M. Jeffreys, William Robins, and also a man by the name of Sam Davies travelled to this inaugural convention. Robins states that during the convention Jeffreys was baptised in water.[63] Amongst the 500 in attendance were some 120 visitors who had travelled from all over Britain to attend the conference.[64] Among them was Pastor W. O. Hutchinson who would found the Apostolic Faith Church in Bournemouth.[65] Smith Wigglesworth was present at these meetings, as was Pastor Hodges from Hereford, testifying to God's healing power.[66] Pastor Calvin Bythol, of the Tabernacle, Brynmawr, recalls his grandfather Charles Noble had travelled to Sunderland from South Wales on his motorcycle. In Pentecostal terms there were to be some significant visitors to Sunderland for the conventions that ran from 1908 to 1914, including Pastor D. P. Williams founder of the Apostolic Church,

---

[61] *Confidence* Issue 2, 10.

[62] *Confidence* Issue 1.

[63] Appendix 1 Testimony of William Robbins.

[64] *Confidence* Issue 4 July 1908 <http://pentecostalarchives.org>.

[65] James E. Worsfold, *The Origins of the Apostolic Church in Great Britain with a Breviate of its Early Missionary Endeavours* (Wellington: Julian Literature Trust, 1991), 34.

[66] *Confidence* Issue 3 June 1908 <http://pentecostalarchives.org>.

Howard Carter and Donald Gee influential in the founding of the Assemblies of God in Great Britain and Ireland, and also George Jeffreys founder of the Elim Pentecostal Church.

After the first convention, William Robins tells how the power of God was very much evident in the train carriage as he returned to Wales. Pastor Hodges remarked; 'What is happening to me now. Can you see oil running down my face?' as oil began to run down from his head, a remarkable occurrence that Robins himself had experienced first-hand.[67]

The distribution of 'Confidence' and the increase in correspondents helped Pentecostals stay in touch and reveals how the Pentecostal work was clearly growing.

T. M. Jeffreys writes following the convention:

> Since returning from Sunderland, God has been leading us along very tenderly. "He knoweth our frame," and so, with great carefulness, He gently leads us to places of securer rest and peace. I am finding Him to be a deep peace and so are others.[68]

In his correspondence to Boddy, Jeffreys also describes how, following the Sunderland convention, the congregation at Waunlwyd had seen the emergence of the 'gift of prophecy' which he then described in detail. In addition to his correspondence, Jeffreys also wrote a number of articles and reports which appeared in 'Confidence' during its publication.

---

[67] Appendix 1 Testimony of William Robbins.
[68] *Confidence* Issue 3, 3.

In January 1909 Alexander Boddy and Cecil Polhill with others formed the Pentecostal Missionary Union (PMU). The purpose was primarily for the training and sending of missionaries to foreign fields, but also for the arranging of Bible training schools. After setting up an executive council, a request was made to the Pentecostal centres around Britain to each provide a representative for the General Council of the PMU.[69] Seen as a Pentecostal Centre, Waunlwyd is identified in South Wales as such by 'Confidence', we find T. M. Jeffreys listed as a member of the General Council and Secretary for the PMU in Wales.[70]

In 1909 Jeffreys travelled as the special representative of PMU to the Pentecostal conference taking place in Mülheim-on-Rhor, Germany. Travelling via Amsterdam, Jeffreys visited a Pastor and Mrs. Polman, who had also been present at Sunderland in 1908, and also meeting their Dutch Pentecostal group. The Pentecostal Conference in Germany was a considerable gathering with some 1400 delegates; Jeffreys wrote enthusiastically about the whole event.[71]

Of note, in 1910 Jeffreys spent a month on mission to Caesarea in Cappadocia, before returning to Europe to obtain three missionaries for the work. He became critically ill with malaria during his travels and whilst in Germany his wife was sent for.

---

[69] *Confidence* Volume 2 Issue 1 January 1909, 13–14<http://pentecostal archives.org>.
[70] *Confidence* Volume 2 Issue 4 April 1909, 80 <http://pentecostalarchives.org>.
[71] *Confidence* Volume 2 Issue 8 August 1909, 189–192 <http://pentecostal archives.org>.

Pastor Niblock writes:

> He went down to the very gates of death. But the Saints held on, and though, at one point, all seemed hopeless and death imminent, the Lord prevailed. Hallelujah!

And so it was that Jeffries had his own remarkable experience of God's life preserving, healing power.[72]

This Congregational minister was the pastor of a small chapel, in a little mining village, found in a corner of South Wales and yet having been baptised with the Holy Spirit, we find him amongst the Spiritual giants of early Pentecostalism. He was very much involved, in the early Pentecostal work, alongside Niblock, Polhill and many others,[73] ministering at the Sunderland Conference in 1908[74] and also at Pentecostal conferences around Britain with such as Cecil Polhill and Smith Wigglesworth. Travelling abroad, as well as extensively at home, something beyond the reach of most village church ministers in the early 1900s. Although often mentioned in the writings of Pentecostal historians, Thomas Madog Jeffries appears overshadowed by the men he stood alongside; yet without doubt he was a founding father of Pentecostalism in South Wales. The men he influenced would themselves have a marked effect on the formation of Pentecostal churches across South Wales.

---

[72] *Confidence* Volume 3 Issue 9 September 1910, 204 <http://pentecostal archives.org>.

[73] *Confidence* Volume 3 Issue 2 February 1910, 95 <http://pentecostal archives.org>.

[74] *Confidence* June 1908 pages 10–11 (http://pentecostalarchives.org).

In 1915 he left Waunlwyd to become minister of the Tabernacle, English Speaking Congregational Church, Aberdare[75] before moving into local politics in 1919.[76] Although there are various local news articles relating to his ministerial activities, sadly, after moving to Aberdare, there is no longer any evidence of Jeffreys continuing to be involved with Pentecostalism.

---

[75] *The Aberdare Leader* 6th February 1915 <http://newspapers.library.wales>.
[76] *The Aberdare Leader* 8th March 1919 <http://newspapers.library.wales/>.

Brynmawr

There were now the beginnings of a Pentecostal group at Brynmawr, in the family home of a Mr. and Mrs. Morris. Around 1911 Price Davies and a colleague Arthur Davies from Aberavon were holding services at the Morris' home. There was an outpouring of the Holy Spirit in Brynmawr at this time.[77] A number of people came to faith at these meetings and were baptised in the Heathcoat pond near the Morris' residence. They were also being baptised with the Holy Spirit.

Due to the attention this caused in the local community, they became known mockingly as the 'Pentecostal dancers'. As in other places, persecution followed, particularly for the younger members. One of the Morris children, Ephraim, would in later years be involved with others in the formation of Apostolic churches around the locality. Another noteworthy name amongst this early Pentecostal group was Charles Noble.[78]

By now the Apostolic Faith Church, founded by W. O. Hutchinson in Bournemouth, was experiencing challenges as differences began to appear between Hutchinson and his Welsh associates. Pastor D. P. Williams, founder of the Apostolic Church, had been much involved with Hutchinson and the Apostolic Faith Church from 1910 until he, with other South Wales leaders, parted company with the Apostolic Faith Church.

---

[77] Gee, *The Pentecostal Movement*, 71.

[78] E. G. Evans, "Monmouthshire Memories: A Brief Account of the Inception of the Apostolic Church in the Monmouthshire Valleys" *Apostolic Herald*: January, February, March 1972).

From this breakaway group of churches emerged the 'Apostolic Church' in South Wales in 1916, with their centre in Penygroes, Carmarthenshire. It was here that they held their first convention in a one thousand capacity tent in 1917.[79]

Brothers Daniel Powell Williams & Jones Williams (standing).

---

[79] Worsfold, *The Origins of the Apostolic Church*, 184.

War

In 1914 Britain entered into the Great War (World War 1) which would last until 11th November 1918. There was considerable difference of opinion amongst early Pentecostals, between those in support of Britain's involvement in the conflict and those who were pacifist.[80] Some prominent Pentecostals such as Howard Carter were imprisoned for their refusal to participate in the conflict. Others such as Donald Gee were forced to work the land in order to support the war effort in an indirect manner.

The Sunderland Conferences and the publication of 'Confidence' now drew to a close. Attention moved instead to London where Cecil Polhill continued holding Pentecostal Conferences under the auspices of the PMU. The PMU would eventually be assimilated into Assemblies of God in 1925 as part of their missionary and training work.[81] The impact of the war was considerable, with British casualties at approximately 1 million deaths and even more wounded, there were very few families unaffected. Dan Williams, in his biography, wrote about his uncle Windsor coming home for Christmas, 1916. He was on furlough from France and the family were so happy at his visit and to see him safe. Sadly, Dan's uncle died later in the war, having been wounded by enemy sniper fire, aged just 19.[82] After the Great War, Britain like much of the world became gripped by great economic depression. Many found themselves out of work or on low wages as the demand for coal,

---

[80] Allen, *The Unfailing Stream*, 121.

[81] Gee, *The Pentecostal Movement*, 51.

[82] D. Williams, *From a Gramp to his Great Grandson: A Grandfathers Testimony* (Tredegar: Paul Beynon, 1997).

iron, and steel declined. In 1973 Ephraim Morris described this period vividly:

> Men and women of half a century ago, who were oppressed by poverty, living in conditions undreamed of today, having no hope in this life, and hitherto knowing nothing of the salvation that Grace had provided. Fifty years ago we shared our bread. We shared our clothes. No man had two suits or pairs of shoes, and more often than not no overcoat, and fortunate to have a second shirt! Money was scarce; many were in debt because of low wages, strikes and lockouts.[83]

The 'boom' of the last decade was over, now with declining demand for coal, iron and steel many found themselves in desperate times and out of work.[84] One of William Robins' grandchildren tells of how one day at work, Robins noticed his brother's name on a list of men to be 'laid off' and having some small income from a family chip shop he went and spoke to the manager and insisted he would take his brothers place. Of course with money scarce it wasn't long before the chip shop suffered too. Arthur Gray-Jones in his *History of Ebbw Vale* estimates by 1931 a third of the male workforce were unemployed and four thousand people had migrated from the area. So dramatic was the effect of the economic depression. In Blaenavon, Ephraim Morris estimated there were three thousand men out of work in 1925.[85]

---

[83] Appendix 2 Testimony of Ephraim Morris (1973)
[84] Gray-Jones, *A History of Ebbw Vale*, 197–200.
[85] Letter from Ephraim Morris to *Apostolic Herald*.

A Coming Together

Jacob Purnell was a young organist at Zoar Baptist Church, Beaufort. He had been saved at the age of thirteen. Around 1917–18 he heard the distinct call of God to 'Leave this place and go to where he did not know'. He accepted this was God directing him to leave Zoar Church and begin seeking after God for where He wanted him. In Ebbw Vale there was a Holiness Mission group meeting, they would later to become an Assemblies of God church.[86]

The Holiness Mission, or churches, had emerged primarily from the Wesleyan and Primitive Methodist Church, promoting 'holiness' and seeking greater spirituality.[87] Although this was not where God was directing Purnell, it was whilst attending meetings there that he met Charles Noble. Charles Noble now introduced Jacob to the Pentecostal house group in Brynmawr. Later this would also prove not to be the place God was directing Jacob either.

During Easter 1918 a Pentecostal mission was held at Zion Baptist Church, Brynmawr. The speaker was none other than Pastor Stephen Jeffreys, himself a man greatly impacted by Evan Roberts during the 1904 Welsh Revival and also by Price Davies.[88] Amongst those attending were Jacob Purnell, Ephraim Morris, Charles Noble, his brother David, and James Seaborne. A number of these would become involved in the growth of the Apostolic Church in the Monmouthshire area. During these meetings James Seaborne

---

[86] K. Thomas, *Faces and Places of Ebbw Vale* (Kerin, 1987).

[87] G. Parrinder, *A Concise Encyclopaedia of Christianity* (Oxford: One World, 1998).

[88] Davies, *The Beginning of the Pentecostal Movement.*

received the Baptism of the Holy Spirit.[89] After his baptism with the Holy Spirit, James spoke about the experience to his brother Thomas. God was moving men into place!

Thomas invited his brother James to hold meetings in his home with Purnell, Morris and the Noble brothers. Thomas lived in the small village of Tafarnaubach near Tredegar. At the meetings Thomas experienced an 'anointing', his wife Mary was baptised with the Holy Spirit and her brother James Meale came to faith and accepted Jesus as his Saviour and went on to become a Pentecostal minister located near Taunton. As things progressed this group of believers, with others, began to hold meetings in the home of Charles Noble at Brynmawr. Amongst them was Charles Bennet who in later years would become one of the elders of the Brynmawr Apostolic Church.[90]

---

[89] Appendix 3 Testimony of Thomas T Seabourne (Circa. 1970).
[90] Evans, "Monmouthshire Memories."

Pastor Frank Hodges

In August 1918 Pastor Frank Hodges from Hereford visited the Apostolic Church convention at Penygroes, West Wales, having heard about the Apostolic Church. The following year he invited Pastor D. P. Williams and other Apostolic pastors to minister in the Hereford church. After this, and conversations regarding doctrinal beliefs, he and the congregation in Hereford joined with the Apostolic Church. Many other meetings were opened, with calls to link up with the Apostolic Church coming from 'so many places' in the surrounding areas.[91]

The market town of Abergavenny was one such location. It is generally believed that the first Apostolic Church in the

---

[91] Apostolic Church UK <http://apostolic-church.org/about-us/history/>.

Monmouthshire Valleys began in Abergavenny. Though details are few, there were a group of believers already meeting in Abergavenny at a Gospel Hall Mission in Mill Street. During his travels by train from Hereford Pastor Hodges would pass through the market town of Abergavenny. It is reckoned that on one occasion, having stopped in the town, Pastor Hodges noticed or was made aware of the meeting place of these believers and contact was made with them, although this account cannot be verified.

It was also during this period that Pastor Hodges and his wife were visiting the group of believers in Brynmawr. Whilst visiting the group, although at that time not attached to the Apostolic Church, he set them in order as a church Assembly. He appointed Charles Noble as the overseer, Jacob Purnell as an evangelist and David Noble as a Deacon.[92]

As the group in Brynmawr continued they held meetings in the home of David Noble, also at Brynmawr. They were now conducting themselves as a church. They were 'tithing,' which is the practise of donating a tenth of one's income to God. Also, the gifts of the Holy Spirit were in use amongst them, particularly prophecy. This led to differences among the group, the question in particular was whether a prophetic utterance should be obeyed. After meeting to discuss these issues, they were unable to resolve the matter and the group split.[93]

---

[92] Evans, "Monmouthshire Memories."
[93] Appendix 3 Testimony of Thomas T Seabourne (Circa. 1970).

The question of prophecy and the acceptance of the gift for directive revelation was one that divided many Pentecostals. Donald Gee commenting on the gift states;

> The thing can be innocent enough so long as the use of such spiritual gifts does not take on a directive character in private or church affairs.'[94]

By comparison, D. P. Williams attributes directive prophecy as instrumental in the development of the Apostolic Church. Writing about the gift of prophecy he makes the following statement:

> "If we are called as an Apostolic Church to witness for something above another, we witness to the unassailable truth that we are a standing Body that is evidence of the existence and value of the prophetic ministry".[95]

Jacob Purnell also wrote of the importance of prophetic ministry (direction) in his own experience,[96] as did many of those who were involved in the early beginnings of the Apostolic Church in the Monmouthshire Valleys.[97]

The Brynmawr group continued, eventually moving into the Tabernacle, Brynmawr. The Tabernacle and a building in Nantyglo were built by local mine owner Mervin Davies. Charles Noble went on to be their pastor, the group later joining with the Assemblies of God. His grandson recalls he had responsibility for the AoG

---

[94] Gee, *The Pentecostal Movement,* 76.
[95] Williams, *The Prophetical Ministry*, 100.
[96] Apostolic Church, *Souvenir* (see also Appendix 4).
[97] Appendix 2 Testimony of Ephraim Morris (1973)

churches at Sirhowy, Brynmawr, and Nantyglo. Price Davies and Arthur Davies were also of considerable influence in these works.[98]

JACOB PURNELL,
Apostle, Monmouthshire District, Wales;
Member of the Council of the A.C.I.B. School.

Pastor Jacob Purnell

---

[98] Gee, Donald. *The Pentecostal Movement*, 71.

Jacob Purnell, Ephraim Morris, and Thomas and James Seaborne, started meeting in the week at Thomas' home in Tafarnaubach. These meetings brought persecution from locals. Thomas' granddaughter remembered her father telling of one man pulling the curtain out through an open window and setting it alight whilst shouting "Fire! Fire!" to disrupt the meeting. The group then began holding meetings in a borrowed chapel, Sardis known as 'Jim John's' Chapel, at Beaufort.

Jacob Purnell's home at Beaufort was also used for meetings on Sunday evenings. In addition to this the group began holding open air meetings. During one of those early meetings, in South Street Beaufort, they were called into the home of a man who had been drinking. By the early hours of the morning the man was saved, and so Mr. William Porter became their first convert in Beaufort. His grandson remembers the account, that on hearing the men preaching outside, he had told his wife, 'invite them in Annie, that's the religion for me.' This man's next door neighbour, also a born again believer, left the Wesleyan Church he attended and joined the group, inviting them to hold meetings in his home. Pastor Hodges and his wife continued to visit the group at Beaufort providing teaching and ministry.[99]

In 1917 an Apostolic church had started in Dowlais under the leadership of Isaac Roberts.[100] Purnell, Morris, and the Seabourne brothers went to an Easter convention being held there. Pastor J. J. Williams and Pastor James Forward were the preachers at this

---

[99] Evans, "Monmouthshire Memories."
[100] Worsfold, *The Origins of the Apostolic Church*, 169.

convention.[101] Whilst there the group asked about the Apostolic Church and were advised to contact the headquarters at Penygroes.[102]

That summer they headed to the 1921 Apostolic International Convention at Penygroes. Money was short, so the group travelled by bicycle — a journey in excess of fifty miles up and down the mountains of the South Wales valleys! On route Jacob Purnell's brakes failed and he began to shout to the others for help. They misheard his cries and thought he was shouting 'Hallelujah!' and so shouted 'Hallelujah' back all the more. Fortunately, there was no accident and he managed to stop safely.[103]

In a conversation with Pastor D. P. Williams the group enquired about the 'Apostolic Vision.'[104] While at Penygroes they heard that some of the pastors from Penygroes were going to Abergavenny to hold meetings over a weekend. Jacob was promised a visit on one evening during the mission to Abergavenny.[105] This was far from good enough for Jacob who began to hatch his own plans. Without the knowledge of the Apostolic pastors, Jacob Purnell had posters printed announcing that an Apostolic Convention was to be held that same weekend at the Sardis Chapel in Beaufort.

A group of possibly six or seven from Abergavenny had also attended the Apostolic convention in Penygroes. In addition, there had been direction through prophecy and interpretation of tongues.

---

[101] Appendix 3 Testimony of Thomas T Seabourne (Circa. 1970)
[102] Evans, "Monmouthshire Memories."
[103] Appendix 3 Testimony of Thomas T Seabourne (Circa. 1970)
[104] Apostolic Church, *Souvenir* (see also appendix 4).
[105] Gordon Weeks, *Chapter Thirty-Two* (Barnsley: Gordon Weeks, 2003), 67.

Both utterances were to the effect that the group should join with the Apostolic Church.[106] The *Apostolic Herald* records that requests to join the Apostolic church from both Abergavenny and Beaufort groups were brought to an Apostles meeting in Penygroes in August 1921.[107] It is clear from the discussions that took place regarding Abergavenny and Beaufort that the two locations were handled together and that the Apostolic leaders saw the locations as being linked to the work of Pastor Frank Hodges from Hereford. In the meeting, the leaders of the Apostolic Church, noted that the request was expressly to join with the Welsh brothers as part of the Apostolic Church. Whilst they had been supported by Pastor Frank Hodges from Hereford, Jacob Purnell had written to Pastor D. P. Williams expressing a desire to be directly included in the Welsh Apostolic Church rather than by connection through Hereford. Until 1922 early Apostolic Church publications listed churches in England as in cooperation and fellowship with the Apostolic Church.[108]

---

[106] Minutes of the Meeting of the Apostles & Elders at Babell, Penygroes, 3rd August 1921 (translated from Welsh).

[107] *Apostolic Herald* 1935.

[108] Worsfold, *The Origins of the Apostolic Church,* 170.

48

Becoming Apostolic

It was on a Saturday that the pastors from Penygroes, D. P. Williams, Jones Williams, Omri Jones, and T. Jones were travelling by train to Abergavenny.[109] They arrived at Beaufort station where they were met by Jacob Purnell. He showed them the poster for a convention at Beaufort that same weekend, which read: 'Apostolic Church Convention at Sardis.' The Penygroes men were perplexed, they went into the old waiting room on the station, and Pastor D. P. Williams (Dan) sought an answer from God through the prophet, Jones Williams. The direction that God gave them was that Pastors D. P. and Jones Williams should remain at Beaufort, and that Pastor Omri Jones and T Jones should go on to Abergavenny. You might say, the first Apostolic meeting held in Beaufort was in that waiting room at the station.[110]

By now the group were eleven including two women. Together with Pastors 'Dan' and Jones Williams they gathered together on the Sunday afternoon at Sardis Chapel. The 'Apostle' Pastor 'Dan' explained the beliefs and 'tenets' of the Apostolic Church. He then invited those present who wished to join the Apostolic Church to respond. Seven accepted, including Jacob Purnell,[111] and so the Apostolic Church in Beaufort was formed. During those meetings, through a prophetic word, Jacob Purnell was appointed as pastor to lead the group and Ephraim Morris was recognised as a prophetic channel.[112]

---

[109] Weeks, *Chapter Thirty-Two*, 67–68.
[110] Evans, "Monmouthshire Memories."
[111] Apostolic Church, *Souvenir* (see also Appendix 4).
[112] Evans, "Monmouthshire Memories."

During the same weekend, the Abergavenny group also joined the Apostolic church under the leadership of overseer Mr. W. C. Williams. By July 1922, Abergavenny and Beaufort were listed in *Riches of Grace* as Apostolic assemblies in Wales.[113] The earliest recollections of Abergavenny church were of meetings held in Mill Street. In the cellar below the meeting place was an area used by residents of the street for laundry. Harry Evans, the leading elder, recalls this was far from ideal as the conversations and bad language of those below could be heard by those above during the services. Those who can remember agree, the congregation at Abergavenny was made up of mostly older people.[114]

In Beaufort the group now began to hold Sunday meetings in Beaufort Hill primary school, having sought permission from the local authority at the advice of Pastor D. P. Williams. News began to spread about these 'Apostolics' and the 'strange things' which went on in their meetings, local gossip caused quite a stir. Many began to come, more out of curiosity and to mock than out of any genuine interest. Some stood on the bank of the old tip at the back of the school to try and watch, others daring to enter the classroom where the meeting was being held. Many ran out at the sound of speaking in tongues, others, hearing the prophetic word of God through Ephraim Morris, stayed; a number who had come out of curiosity began to attend regularly. Jacob Purnell wrote of the early days at the school, 'it was more like a side show than anything else.'[115]

---

[113] *Riches of Grace* Volume 2 No. 2 (July 1922).
[114] Appendix 5 Brief Recollections by Harry Evans (2015).
[115] Apostolic Church, *Souvenir* (see also Appendix 4).

Pastor W. James of Pontardawe visited Beaufort for about three months to assist the group with the work. Isaac Roberts and others from Dowlais also provided much support and would travel to help with the meetings at Tafarnaubach.[116] In the November, whilst holding Sunday night house meetings in Beaufort, a frail woman suffering with terrible nerves came and asked for prayer. She accepted Jesus as her saviour and Lord and from that time on she was dramatically changed, immediately testifying of her salvation. Within three weeks her husband was also attending the meetings, having seen the change in his wife. One evening, as Pastor Purnell gave an appeal 'who will receive Christ?' the man replied 'I'll have him, Jake.' The man was Phillip Williams a notorious drunkard and well-known bare knuckle fighter from the locality.[117] Philip Williams would eventually be ordained as a Pastor in the Apostolic church.

The classroom soon became too small, gradually they began to need increasingly larger rooms. Whatever the reason, people were coming and God was saving them! Members of other churches also began to come along to the meetings held on Sunday evenings. This made them unpopular with the conventional churches, but the people were hungry for an encounter with God. The unchurched of all types, drunkards, gamblers, the profane, were coming to faith. Those present testified to many healings, people suffering from consumption, those who were crippled and the mute were all healed. Many more were baptised with the Holy Spirit, speaking in other tongues and some prophesying. A formal program began to

---

[116] Evans, "Monmouthshire Memories."
[117] Philip J. Williams, *The Touch of the Masters Hand* (Bradford: Puritan Press, 1954).

be established, Sundays at Beaufort Primary School, Mondays and Saturdays at 'Jim John's' Chapel, and on Thursdays in the home of one of the members.

From just seven people the work had grown rapidly so that by 1923 the Beaufort Apostolic assembly had eighty members. With the addition of visitors and regular attenders, the Sunday evening meetings were now attracting between 200 and 300 people.[118]

Pastor PHILIP WILLIAMS, Beaufort, Mon.

---

[118] Apostolic Church, *Souvenir* (see also appendix 4).

During a visit by Pastors T. Rees and Omri Jones, Philip Williams and Thomas Seabourne were appointed as elders in the Beaufort assembly. It is clear that there was a fresh revival experience taking place at Beaufort amongst these Apostolic Pentecostals.

With the growth of the work there was an increasing need for their own building in which to meet and hold services. An old building was found, previously it had been a stable and now was being used as a rag store. With the help of the Penygroes ministers who were responsible for buildings, the purchase was arranged. The building was fully renovated and through prophecy this new church was named 'Bethel.' In April 1923 the building was opened as Bethel church, much to the delight of the congregation.[119] The following week thirty-two people were baptised in water, a week later more were baptised. Amongst those baptised were, Thomas Seabourne and his wife, and also his brother James.[120]

With a permanent building much progress could occur, on Tuesday evenings the assembly began meetings for the children, teaching choruses and encouraging the older ones to prepare a small sermon on a given Bible text. It was here at the age of twelve that a young Danny Williams, son of Philip Williams, gave his first sermon in front of Pastor Purnell.[121]

---

[119] Evans, "Monmouthshire Memories."

[120] Appendix 3 Testimony of Thomas T Seabourne (Circa. 1970)

[121] Williams, *From a Gramp to his Great Grandson.*

A very early photo of the first congregation at 'Bethel' Beaufort (c.1924)

Expansion

In the early days the work was prolific, many churches were started or contact made with existing unaffiliated Pentecostal groups. Those who agreed with the Apostolic Tenets of Belief, subsequently chose to join the Apostolic Church. As the members of the Beaufort Assembly began to start house meetings or hold outreach campaigns in their own neighbourhoods, new works began to appear, others relocating for work carried the vision with them.

Later in 1923 a prophetic word was given for elder Phillip Williams to move with his family, from Beaufort, to his mother's house in Ebbw Vale. This required sacrifice, as the family had just been offered a new place to live in Beaufort. However, in obedience to the prophetic word, they moved. Phil Williams now began to hold house meetings at his mother's home in Newtown, and so the Apostolic Church in Ebbw Vale began. By 1924 they were renting a meeting room in the local market hall. There was only one other man assisting Phil in those early days and so his son Danny also helped. He would hand out hymn books and tend to the fire, in those days the rooms were still heated by coal fire or stove.[122] Around this time young Danny Williams began working with his father down the 'pit.' He tells of how Phil Williams would 'wait on God' for his ministry whilst working the coalface before coming home to preach at that evening's service.

---

[122] Williams, *The Touch of the Masters Hand*.

Retired Elder John Pratton recalls his grandmother had gone to the market hall, babe in arms, to buy bread. She was told, 'go on in there Mrs. you'll get bread,' as she was ushered into the church meeting. She was saved in the meeting, and as a result in later years a number of her family members have served God in the Apostolic Church.

By 1925 the Ebbw Vale Assembly moved and began holding meetings in Pontygoff Girls School, sat at the desks in one of the classrooms. An amusing account is told of a particularly large lady who had come to the services at Pontygoff. A prophecy was given to the effect that 'you will not leave the desk until you have given your heart to the Lord.' When the lady went to get up at the end of the meeting, she was firmly stuck. Remarkably, she committed her life to Jesus and was immediately able to rise from the desk.

As a result of the outreach from the Beaufort assembly, it was not long before there was an 'Apostolic' group meeting in Brynmawr. This congregation were holding meetings in a room above the India and China Tea Shop in Beaufort Street. The meeting place was endearingly referred to as 'the upper room.' Those who were children at the time still recall Charles Bennett leading the group.[123]

Returning to events in Waunlwyd, the Pentecostal members that had been with T. M. Jeffreys at the Tabernacle, were now meeting in a local house. There is little information regarding how this began; however, given Jeffreys' comments regarding persecution,[124] it is possible to suggest that following Jeffreys' relocation to Aberdare the group faced increasing opposition from non-

---

[123] Appendix 5 Brief Recollections by Harry Evans (2015).
[124] *Confidence* Issue 1, 2.

Pentecostals at Tabernacle. Whatever the cause, the Pentecostals had now become a separate congregation in Waunlwyd. During the 1920s this group, who were amongst the first Pentecostals in Wales, made the decision to join with the Apostolic Church. Amongst them were William Robins and his wife; Robins would be recognised as an elder in the local leadership.

As a product of the Pentecostal groups that sprang up as a direct result of the Waunlwyd 'outpouring,' there was a small Pentecostal church meeting in Llanhilleth. The Apostolic work was spreading and an Apostolic work was also planted in the locality. One of the founding members was Ivor Bevan who left the Presbyterian church to join the 'Apostolics'. Ivor Bevan's daughter recalls how Pastor Omri Jones, who was working in the area at the time, came and set the assembly in order. Ivor's wife, Phylis May, was not willing to follow him and join the Apostolic church. However, when their five-year-old son had fallen and was severely injured, Phylis put out a 'fleece'. 'Lord if my boy recovers I'll join the Apostolic church,' sure enough their son recovered and she joined the Apostolic church. By the late 1940s the early Llanileth independent Pentecostal church came to a close and the few remaining members joined with the Llanileth Apostolic church.

Pastor Purnell and church members outside the Llanhileth church building.

In 1923 a group in Blaenafon had started meeting as a result of Pentecostal mission into the locality. Having been left with no leader contact was made by men from the Beaufort Apostolic assembly; amongst whom was Ephraim Morris. In 1925 Pastor T. Rees and Prophet Omri Jones came to Blaenafon to formally establish the church, appointing local leaders to oversee the assembly, by which time there were some thirty people meeting regularly. They were meeting in a church building hired from the Seventh Day Adventists. People were being baptised in water, and receiving the baptism with the Holy Spirit, there were also healings taking place in Blaenafon. Among the more notable, Ephraim Morris writes of a blind man having his sight restored and a large tumour, the size of a walnut, completely disappearing from a woman's wrist![125]

---

[125] Letter from Ephraim Morris to *Apostolic Herald*.

Rev. Dennis Porter the grandson of the William Porter who had been saved in Beaufort, recounts how the family moved to Pontllanfraith where William began working at the Wylie colliery. The colliery began to produce coal in 1926.[126] He now commenced an Apostolic work in Pontllanfraith. Eventually William Porter opened a fish shop in the locality and raised sufficient funds to purchase a plot of ground. The Pontllanfraith church first met in a tin hut there, in later years enough money was raised to build a brick building.

In time another work commenced in the village of Cwm near Ebbw Vale; the meetings were held above a local shop in Marine Street. The group that started there included the Owens brothers, with William Robins also being involved in the opening of the Cwm Church.

In Rassau a new work emerged, this group began to hold meetings at 'Strouds', a local milk and dairy supplier. In 1931 the group were recognised as an Apostolic Assembly.[127] The congregation moved to a second location, in another dairy, before eventually moving into their own building in 1938.

One of the highlights for Pastor Jacob Purnell was the fulfilment of prophecy given in 1923 and 1931, this was realised when he became pastor in Newport in 1932. It is generally accepted that Pastor Frank Hodges had made contact with a Pentecostal group in Newport who subsequently joined the Apostolic Church. Jacob Purnell writes that

---

126 <www.welshcoalmines.co.uk/Gwent/Wyllie.htm>
127 Weeks, *Chapter Thirty-Two*, 126,

by 1933 there were three church assemblies established in Newport and the work was 'advancing.'[128]

The work of the Apostolic groups was spreading quickly south down the valleys. A work was begun in Six Bells between Abertillery and Llanhileth. During the 1930s, for a short period, there was a mission work in Sirhowy. In Brithdir a work began in 1940, this group would eventually move to Bargoed. By 1950 there was also work for a short time in Clydach near Abergavenny. There is recollection of a second assembly in Ebbw Vale for a short period, when the local synagogue in Briery Hill was given to the Apostolic Church. There was a tremendous missional attitude amongst these early 'Apostolics.' Missions, church groups or outreaches were opened in many locations including Pontypool, Ystrad Mynach, Fleur De Llys, and Cwmfelinfach. When Ephraim Morris wrote about the opening of the Blaenafon Assembly, he was already mentioning their aspiration to begin a work in Abersychan.[129] Jacob Purnell was a prolific evangelist, it would almost seem that if he were waiting for a bus that was delayed, he would plant a church whilst he was waiting!

---

[128] Apostolic Church, *Souvenir* (see also appendix 4).
[129] Letter from Ephraim Morris to *Apostolic Herald*.

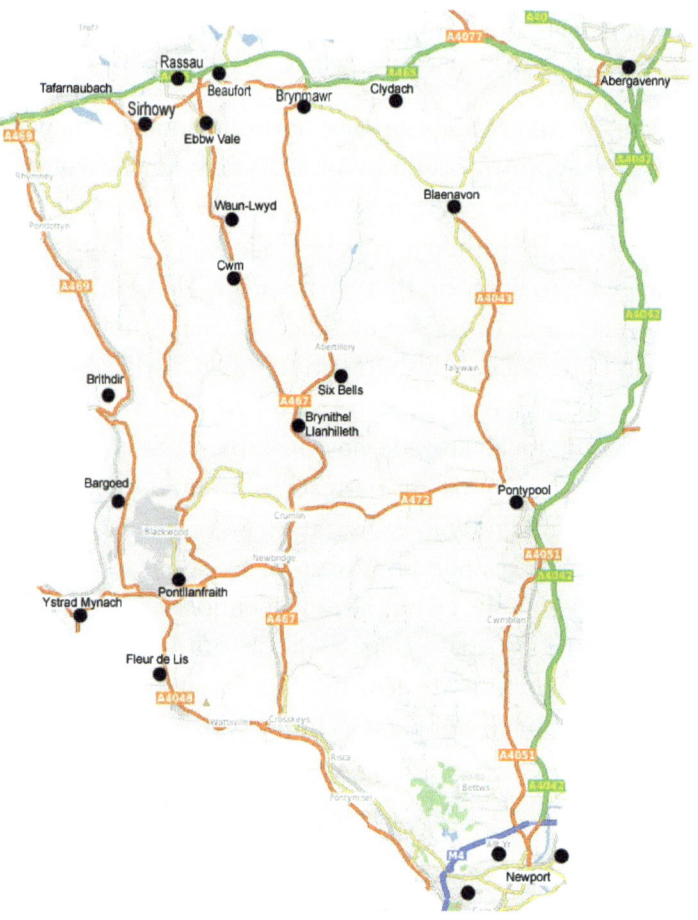

General locations of Apostolic Church expansion in the Monmouthshire Valleys

Apostolic Church Life

In the early days there was a very high standard expected of members within the Apostolic Church. The congregations were segregated, men on one side and the women on the other. A dress code was also kept, women wore hats, no trousers and skirts had to reach below the knee. Men also were expected to dress in a sober and appropriate manner, the Sunday suit being preferable where it could be afforded. Pastor Phil Williams recounts his experiences during the 'great depression.' Having no good shirt to wear for 'chapel' he had prayed. Whilst walking across the hills from Ebbw Vale to Beaufort he saw a shirt being blown across the grass. He picked it up, and with no one coming forwards to claim it, he trusted this was a gift of providence from God. Sure enough when he tried it on, it was a perfect fit.[130] This dress code was sometimes taken to the extreme. For example, the story is told that in Abergavenny during the Second World War, there was a young lady who played the organ. She was working for the land army, as did many women in that period. The lady had arrived at church straight from work, not having had time to return home and change from her work fatigues. Sadly, no understanding was shown, she was sternly spoken to about the matter, she never returned.

---

[130] Williams, *The Touch of the Masters Hand.*

The early congregations were born out of mission and strongly committed to local mission and witness. There would be regular marches, followed by singing and preaching meetings; open air campaigns were also an important aspect of outreach. Local congregations would hold processions through the streets known as witness marches, often accompanied by a church band and led by witness banners. These would continue for many years. Of note were the May Day rallies which were rotated each year throughout the three districts.

The New "Witness" Banner.

Jacob Purnell with the new Apostolic witness banner c. 1925

Above & below: Open air outreach Bargoed c. 1960

Above: Witness March, Rassau c.1970s

Above: Witness March, Brynmawr c.1980s

As the work grew and the number of church assemblies increased, the work was organised into three districts. The Monmouthshire valleys were referred to as the Beaufort Area in which were Newport, Ebbw Vale, and Beaufort Districts. Although divided into administrative districts, there was a great deal of unity and support amongst the various congregations within the Beaufort Area. Every form of evangelical activity was undertaken to promote the gospel and win souls for Christ. Gospel Tracts, open air meetings, evangelical crusades were, and continued to be, a significant part of Apostolic mission activity in the locality.

The Rassau 'Sunshine Corner' group circa 1950

Children's work was also given a high priority, with most assemblies holding regular children's activity. Recital of Bible verses, singing of Sunday school songs, and stories from the bible were all part of the work. The annual church and Sunday school trips were a big feature of church life for all involved. One popular destination being Porthcawl. Many of the older church members still delight at the idea of a trip to the beach at Porthcawl, and not forgetting the all-important 'bag of chips'.

As the congregations began to grow in number, there were more members with instruments and musical talents. This led to the formation of a band in Brynmawr under the direction of a former Salvation Army bandmaster.[131] The band would often join in the local witness marches, leading the way, as the congregation followed singing whatever hymn the band was playing. In Brynmawr a choir was also started, which had been encouraged by a prophetic word.

At the time there were electricity shortages and power was cut to non-essential buildings at certain times, so the church rarely had electricity during the midweek evenings to provide light. As a result, an offer was made for the choir to meet in the evening at a local community centre. God was clearly at work with a bigger plan. Now the choir were meeting at the community centre they were listed as an evening class. The county then paid a small wage to the choir leader and also the pianist which they then used to fund transportation for the choir. The choir sang at the Penygroes International convention and also toured throughout the UK.

One central feature of church life that everyone in the locality remembers were the Easter conventions. Easter celebrations were a time for all the local assemblies to gather together in worship and celebration. Memories are of meeting in Zoar Chapel which was borrowed for the convention, the meetings were always packed. When such special services were held in 'Bethel' Beaufort the young people would often have to sit on the window sills and others having to stand throughout the whole meeting. Those who grew up attending these meetings still have a sense of awe in their

---

[131] Appendix 5 Brief Recollections by Harry Evans (2015).

recounting the events of these conventions. People would travel from the other Apostolic assemblies across Monmouthshire in order to attend. The atmosphere was charged with spiritual fervour. With so many choir men present in the gatherings the singing was tremendous. Throughout the whole weekend everyone was in anticipation, expectant for what they would hear through the prophet and from the preacher.

At Whitsun a convention was held in Ebbw Vale and again people would attend from Apostolic Churches all over the Monmouthshire Area. The next convention would take place during August, this time in the Newport District. Over Christmas there would be another convention in Brynmawr. The youth would be responsible for a meeting during the afternoon of the conventions. All these conventions were well attended by members of the Apostolic churches across the three districts of the Beaufort Area.

Travelling to support the various district and area special services was a central part of Apostolic life. There was a unity and support that connected the local assemblies, churches acting as districts and as areas rather than in isolation. Many relationships were formed between young couples from the various church assemblies as they met at the inter-church events. Young men and women would be given opportunities to take part at youth rallies before moving up to take part in special services and so develop in ministry and gifting. Always there was a sense of expectancy and excitement. Pastor Calvin Bythol recollects that as a young man, he came to the 'Apostolics'. 'In those days, they had all the young people' was the comment as to why he joined the Apostolic church.

At Penygroes, during the annual convention, young people would form friendships and relationships with others from across the country. In 1940 as part of the Penygroes Convention a Witness Movement Rally was held. Anne Pritchard from Rassau gave her testimony, as did Mrs. E Collins from Pontypool.[132]

During the late 1940s there was a further move of God amongst the Apostolic churches. Many were saved, including a group of young tearaways, amongst whom were Windsor Davies who would become a pastor in the district and Arthur Dunn who would move to Germany and become the pastor of Flensburg Apostolic Church.

Throughout the twentieth century there were many crusades, festivals, conventions and special services under the various pastors who have led the church districts. Baptismal services were a continuing feature of church activity, as were the countless testimonies of God's saving grace and life changing power.

During the 1980s the Apostolic youth were experiencing a Pentecostal outpouring. Pastor Haydn Twinberrow recalls going to collect his daughters from the Ebbw Vale church after a youth meeting only to find the youth still praising God as the Holy Spirit had descended upon their gathering. This Pentecostal experience of spiritual refreshing has continued; at times the churches have enjoyed much of God's blessing. In some assemblies there have continued to be men and women saved, baptised, filled with the Holy Spirit and accounts of miracles and healings.

---

[132] Apostolic Church. *The Glorious Gospel, Apostolic International Convention* August 1940, 80–82.

Building Works

From the start of the Apostolic Church in the Monmouthshire valleys there was a concerted effort to establish not only a local congregation, but also to purchase or build their own buildings in which to meet.

By 1934 the congregation in Ebbw Vale had raised sufficient money to purchase their own church building. However, the national leadership of the Apostolic Church asked if they could borrow the money in order to build a church in Ystradgynlais. The elders agreed and so their building was delayed until 1935 when Pastor Purnell purchased a plot of ground at Pontygoff, Ebbw Vale and Peniel Church was built. In 1938 the Rassau Assembly raised sufficient funds to build their own church building, 'Moriah' on Rassau Road. The building cost £38 and was constructed by Albert George builders who carried out the building work for the cost of the materials only. The Brynmawr assembly had also been able to arrange sufficient funding to build their own church building, Pastor Jacob Purnell undertaking the arrangements. In 1939 they began meeting in their new building at Clydach Street, Brynmawr.

It must be remembered that during this period there was great financial hardship, many were experiencing periods of unemployment and others were caught in strike action. It is remarkable that the congregations were able to raise sufficient funds to build churches and a tremendous testimony to the sacrificial giving of the people.

By 1950 the assembly in Cwm had raised enough money to build their own building which was opened in Canning Street.

In 1953 the Abergavenny assembly were finding Mill Street unsuitable and arranged the rental of the disused 'Chapel of Rest' on Old Hereford Road. The building had to be completely renovated, the work being carried out by the local men who worked tirelessly to turn a disused building into a spiritual home for the Congregation. In 1956 the Clydach Street building in Brynmawr was sold, leaving the congregation without a building. Fortunately, the church was able to acquire the old Salvation Army building in King Street and continued to meet there. In 1964 the church in Brythdir moved to a new building in Bargoed.

The 1964 opening of the Bargoed Apostolic church building

In 1967 a compulsory purchase order was placed on 'Peniel,' the Ebbw Vale Church building. As a result, the congregation moved into Libanus Road, a former Methodist Chapel, until the building was no longer useable. Sadly, Waunlwyd Assembly went into decline and was closed in the 1970s.

In the early 1980s the Llanhilleth building burned down and the group relocated to neighbouring Brynithel, the meetings being held in the local community hall for a few years before the assembly was closed.

Eventually in 1994 the Ebbw Vale Assembly bought the former Magistrates court and opened as 'the Christian Centre'. Elder Danny Williams, then in his retirement, opened the building at an official ceremony. The Apostolic Church still meets at the Christian Centre today.

The decision was taken to close 'Bethel' church Beaufort in the 1990s, and in 2002 the Cwm church was also closed. Declining attendance was given as the reason for the closures. In 2006 a decision was taken to amalgamate the remaining churches in the Blaenau Gwent County. This resulted in the closure and sale of the Rassau and Brynmawr buildings along with the joining together of their respective congregations at the Christian Centre, Ebbw Vale. In other locations too, church closures became necessary. Today the Apostolic church in what was the Monmouthshire valleys continues. Congregations meet in four locations, the Newport Gateway Church, The Pontllanfraith Church, Abergavenny 'Bethel' Church and the Christian Centre, Ebbw Vale.

A rare photo of the Mill Street Church, Abergavenny

All Saints Parish Hall Monkwearmouth Today

Bethany Apostolic Church Pontllanfraith

Bethany Apostolic Church Abergavenny

Brynmawr Church King Street Building

Blaenafon Church Building

Ebbw Vale Church

Newport Gateway Church

Cwm Church Canning Street Building

Rassau Church Building

Apostolic Ministers

Pastors Jim and Son Mel Seaborne

There has been a rich and continued flow of ministry raised up from amongst the congregations of the Monmouthshire valleys. Individuals have been recognised as apostles, prophets, evangelists, pastors, and teachers; in accordance with the ministries gifts of Ephesians 4:11. Some of the most notable figures being: Jacob Purnell who planted a number of churches in the locality also ministering across the UK and abroad; Ernie Hammond, who served in various senior roles within the denomination; Mel Seabourne, (son of James Seabourne) who served a term as president of the Apostolic Church from 1981–1986; and Paul Howells, originally from the Rhondda, was called into the pastorate and today serves as deputy national leader of the Apostolic Church. There have also been those called as National Prophets such as Howard Chiplin and Hayden Twinberrow. Others have been called into pastoral ministry including Philip Williams, James Seabourne,

Bill Woolridge, Windsor Davies, Peter Williams, Clive Evans, and Selwyn Tiley.

Some of those influenced by the early Apostolic testimony have been used of God in other denominations. David Edwards became a Presbyterian minister in Ebbw Vale. Dennis Porter became an ordained minister as did Byron Jones. Roy Bevans became a pastor in America. Victor Owens was pastor of an independent Pentecostal church in Pontypool. He and his wife now serve as itinerant missionaries traveling to Indonesia and Argentina. Philip Keevil went to Bible College in America before becoming a minister there. Calvin Bythol became the Pastor of Tabernacle Assemblies of God church in Brynmawr.

Pastor Mel Seabourne and family at Albert Seabourne's graveside.

There have been a number of men who along with their wives and families have left to serve abroad on the mission fields these include:

George Purnell, the nephew of Jacob Purnell who became a pastor in the Apostolic church and relocated to Canada, and Albert Seabourne and his wife who were called as missionaries for the Apostolic Church to Ghana (Albert passed away Christmas day 1961 whilst in service on the mission field).

Another who served on the mission field was Tom Ford. There was also Pastor Allan Rees who emigrated with his family to serve in Germany. Arthur Dunn who moved to Flensburg, Germany and became the pastor of the Apostolic church. Pastor Johnathan Edwards and his family were sent to Portugal as missionaries. Granville Johnson and his wife would spend most of their lives on the mission fields of Southern Africa. Granville's brother, Russell moved to Germany where he conducted radio ministry. Peter Keevil and his wife became missionaries in Venezuela before serving in the Apostolic Church as missionaries to Chile. Philip Woolridge, son of Pastor Bill Woolridge, became a pastor before relocating to Chile as a missionary and then moving to Canada to lead a church in Toronto, his wife Rebecca also being recognised there by the Canadian Apostolic church as assistant pastor. Mairwen Bull married an Italian man and left to serve with her husband in Sicily and Italy.

Alongside the many men who have been called into pastoral ministry from the Monmouthshire Valleys, there have been many more who have relocated and faithfully served in the area. The Apostolic churches of the Beaufort Area have been blessed with many good leaders, their wives and families, who have cared for, nurtured and helped in the spiritual development of the congregations. There are many fond memories recounted, many happy moments recalled; and the Apostolic church has been made all the richer for them all.

Beaufort Eldership circa 1934

The amount of spiritual ministry required in the locality would be far too great for a local or district pastor alone. The greater portion of the work was carried out by local laymen, some called as elders, others deacons or deaconesses to each local assembly. The church has been built by members who have stood shoulder to shoulder with the pastors, sharing the burden of the work. The officers of the church have given untold hours and laboured much in God's service, preaching, convening, visiting the congregation, encouraging, and leading their local assemblies. Amongst them, laymen who have led local churches as overseers or non-salaried pastors. Some of these men would work underground, in the steel mill or other professions before coming to convene or preach at evening meetings. Others have served as deacons and deaconesses quietly tending to the needs of each assembly. So whilst Jacob

Purnell is credited with the early beginnings of the work in Monmouthshire, many others have followed him in the various ministries of the Apostolic Church, and the work continues.

Appendix A1

Copy of the Hand Written Testimony of William Robins.

I expect that everybody is acquainted with the fact of the 1904–5 Revival either by experience or hearsay. But at the request of many friends I have promised to recount some of my memories of the outpouring of the Holy Spirit at Waunlwyd. Trusting it may be to the Glory of God, and a help to younger Saints.

The best way I think will be for me to start with my own conversion. I was brought up to attend Sunday school and evening service, having a tendency for that when I was young. I say this because I was not made to go by my parents. So long as I went, I could choose for myself. So I went to various places according to where my companions were going. My mother was a Baptist; my father was nothing. When I was about 13 or 14 years old, there was a prayer meeting being held every morning in a stall road in the colliery, and I loved to be at that prayer meeting. So I would creep up against them on the outside, so that I could hurry away when it was over, for I feared the wrath of my father, if I was not ready to start work when he was. But I longed to be like those men. I thought they were wonderful men. George Harris, Henry Harris, Frank Jones and others. How easy it would have been to lead me to Jesus when my heart was tender had they known.

When I was about 17 years I began to drift into worldly things, and at 18 I was coming home the worse for drink, which nearly broke my mother's heart. Her consolation was that her other two boys would not go astray. At 22 I married which had a steadying effect on me for a while. But I was invited to become secretary of a football club, and that led me back into worldly things and this continued until I was 30 years of age. Now the Revival was on, but in the August of 1904 I was compelled to leave this district through the serious condition of my wife, as she was suffering from neuritis. The doctor calling me aside one day and told me that if I did not take her from here, she would either be in the Asylum or the cemetery.

Her choice was a village near Pontymoile where she had a sister. Now this sister was a member of the Pontymoile Mission Hall (Undenominational) and a very active worker in the Revival meetings. I was induced to attend a service in the mission one Sunday. I had not been to chapel for many years but was convicted at once of my sinfulness. So I determined I would never go there again. But in the mission hall on the second floor was a little room where prayer was frequently made. There was a prayer meeting at 7 o'clock every Sunday morning (the superintendent told me afterwards that it had been held for 27 years without a break). Souls were prayed for in that meeting and I was mentioned as one that should be prayed for. Now I had no desire to be saved, I was enjoying the life I was living, but my sister in law never missed a chance to invite me to the Revival meetings. Being in a bad temper one Thursday night I answered her very viciously. 'If I don't alter my mind I shall never come!' And those were the words that stuck, and I could not get rid of them. When they returned from the meeting, I was sat in the middle of the house with my feet on the fender, my elbows on my knees, my chin cupped in my hands looking into the fire and I had been there all the time they had been away, thinking of those words and the consequence.

The next day I was very quiet, so much so that the little boy that was working with me wanted to know what was the matter, was I ill. 'No Billie I'm alright,' I said. I didn't know it was conviction, all

I know was I didn't want to talk to anyone. Now I come to the remarkable influence of the Holy Spirit. On the Saturday I had intended to do the same as I always did. But instead of calling at all the public houses between Pontypool and the village where I lived, I went straight home. However, I said to my wife, 'now I'll go down to the Unicorn for a drink.' I called for 'a pint of beer,' but the taste was awful. So I said to the landlord, 'what's the matter with your beer tonight Johnson?' 'I have had no complaints from anyone Robins' he said. Then I said to a man sitting by me, 'taste my beer.' 'I see nothing the matter with it,' he said. So I tasted his which tasted the same as mine. I failed to drink it and went home. My wife being flabbergasted as 12 o'clock was my usual time.

On Sunday morning I had a longing to go to the mission hall although I could not understand why. I had many pricks of conscience there that day, which may not interest anyone. But in the evening service I accepted Jesus as my saviour. My wife, my sister in law, and family were rejoicing at my salvation. But I was not happy. The awful responsibility of being a Christian seemed terrible to me. And as soon as I could I left them and went to my own cottage and down on my knees by my armchair and told God how I felt and asked him to make me a real Christian. Then I had the experience of knowing God was in it. A great load went off me and I felt thrilled, and said to myself, 'this is what they mean by being saved!' After we had had our supper that night I took up the Bible and the first words I saw, which seemed to stand out on the page were, 'My Grace is sufficient for thee'. In wonder I turned to my wife and saw she was reading the young soldier, and on the page was a flag with the words, 'My Grace is sufficient for thee'. I accepted that as a token of God's interest in me, and greatly marveled, for God had until then always seemed afar off to me.

Water Baptism

At Whitsun 1908 we went to convention at Sunderland. Our Pastor Mr. Jeffreys was baptised in water (in the sea) and as soon as he rose from the water he came rushing towards me shouting, 'praise God Brother Robins the Lord has given me the same experience'.

The superintendent asked me about water baptism as he was intending to preach two sermons on the subject. Being unable to attend through working afternoons he invited me to read the scriptures about it. By so doing I was soon satisfied that immersion was the scriptural way, and gave my name as a candidate for baptism. It was a great experience to me, coming out of the water I was enveloped by a great heat as if I was in a furnace and began to shout and praise God. I think it was a baptism of fire.

About this time, I had a very unpleasant experience. I got the sack at Blaendare Slope where I was working. I came to see afterwards that it was God's way for me. After being idle for some weeks I saw my old manager at Waunlwyd and was prompted to ask him for work. 'Yes', he said, 'I have been expecting you back a long time.' So I returned to Waunlwyd and joined the Congregational Church. Now in this church the Revival Spirit was still in evidence. The Pastor Mr. J. M. Jeffreys having had a great blessing in the revival had given up school teaching and become a minister. He was a great scholar and a godly man. I think there was a bit of controversy about me between the deacons because of water baptism by immersion, as he approached me on the matter and I told him my experience and did not wish to argue on the point as no amount of argument could rob me of that experience. One Monday evening in September 1906 there was sports in a field nearby. Most people were going to the sports. And the question arose between me and a bosom companion. What should we do? But we decided for the prayer meeting.

We were 3 men, the minister, G. B. and myself, as well as 5 or 6 women. As the meeting progressed I was had a peculiar experience and it proved my brother was having a similar experience. I turning to him and whispered I shall have to go out, I am dying to laugh. With that he burst out and the both of us were laughing and could not stop until I was quite sore around my ribs. So I said Lord if this is of you, stop it, and it stopped immediately. Then my brother stood up and apologised to the pastor and the women claiming it was of God and not of ourselves. Praise God the minister was very patient with us, as he had to be with me for many months, but that demonstration of joy remained with me always, so that to see or mention the name of Jesus would set me off laughing.

About the end of 1906 or early 1907 there was a 12-day mission arranged by Ebbw Vale Free Church Council. It was decided to hold the mission for 6 days in Ebbw Vale, 3 days in Beaufort and 3 days at the lower end, which was Waunlwyd and Victoria. The meetings being held at Bethel Victoria. It was a wonderful time and during the last meeting many were prostrated under the power of God, among them Mr. T. M. Jeffreys our minister and he was laughing. I was glad, if it was only for his patience with me. We come now to October of 1907 when another mission was arranged by the free churches at Waunlwyd and Victoria. I should have said the minister at the previous mission was W. S. Jones, Llewnapin, and having such a blessed time then it was decided to invite him again.

Spirit Baptism

During all these months there had been a question in our hearts and minds at Tabernacle Church. Could we expect an experience according to Acts 2? With much seeking, but everyone afraid to venture seeing no one had yet received this. Well, Rev. W. S. Jones was to minister and everything was going well until the last week when Rev. J. M. Jeffreys who was acting secretary, received a telegram saying Rev. W. S. Jones was ill and could not come. The time being too short now to correspond many others, it was suggested that Rev. W. S. Jones be asked to find a substitute, and then a remarkable thing happened.

There was a pastor from Broadstairs named Niblock that had received a word from God telling him to go to Wales. He had his box packed ready waiting for the word to go, when he received the telegram from W. S. Jones asking him to take his place. One of the first questions we asked Pastor Niblock was: Can we expect a baptism of the Spirit according to Acts 2? 'Yes, of course,' he said. The meetings were a great success, so much so that some wished to continue the mission. Pastor Niblock offered to trust the Lord for his maintenance, but the committee decided against it. So Tabernacle people decided to continue on their own, and commenced tarrying for the baptism in the Holy Spirit. It is impossible for me to describe the awe of the presence of God in those meetings, which were held every night through the week, right on until Christmas. It had been arranged months previously to hold our usual Christmas tree and 'Bran Tub dips' (lucky dip) and £5 had been allotted for toys. The vestry had to be used for the occasion so it was arranged to hold the meeting in a room in the minister's house. This was on Christmas Eve 1907. Now there was much persecution from Christian people and others including family, and it is necessary for me to refer to one case. John Jones faced opposition from his wife and this particular night she had hid his shoes to stop him to come to the meeting. So not to be beat he went to the recess under the stairs and got an old pair of 'slaps' and come in them. That night John spoke in tongues. I won't describe the meeting, but the news went like wildfire. Next day the meetings commenced in the morning continued all day. Many others receiving the Baptism speaking in tongues. The people all wondering many declaring we had gone mad, and the persecution becoming intensified, many driven to search their Bibles. One minister preached a sermon on the text, 'tongues shall cease'. About this time my wife as I have mentioned before was healed of her neuritis; many others were healed and demons were cast out.

Now may I describe some of my own experience. All through this wonderful time we were very busy in the Lord's work. Open airs, cottage prayer meetings, tract distribution, every house in the village receiving a tract every Sunday morning, with the brethren not worrying about their natural food, so we would go to bed feeling very tired. Even so, we would start to laugh and rise in the morning quite refreshed.

One night as we were kneeling in prayer, it was as if a sheet was thrown over me, but fear gripped me and it went away. Oh how I was tormented of the devil all next day. 'You have grieved the Holy Spirit and he will not bother with you again'. But I prayed and cried unto God for forgiveness. Praise his name! The same experience came again the next night, which I welcomed and told the Lord to have his way with me. Then I felt as if oil were poured on my head and ran down my neck and down my face to the end of my nose and chin, and then back again. And for several years when I went to shave a weight would come on my head as if a hand was placed lightly upon it. I still have it even as I am writing this testimony. Now 40 years have passed and the blessed Lord has been very precious all along, and is still precious. And I pray that this testimony may be to His glory, and a help to younger saints seeking the Lord. Amen.

I would to mention here, I had often prayed that God would give this wonderful experience to someone. There were 4 returning in the train from Sunderland: Pastor Jeffreys, Pastor Hodges, Sam Davies and myself. When Pastor Hodges began to say. What is happening to me now. Can you see oil running down my face? It's like that he said.

Another incident in the train that had an amusing side. The train was standing in the platform at Leeds. A young man got in and threw his cap on the rack and opened a newspaper. In a few minutes he said, 'I must go from here,' 'There is no need' I said, 'there's plenty of room.' So he proceeded to read the paper. But in a few minutes he jumped up, took his cap off the rack and hurried out of the compartment.

Healings

I will mention a few of the healings we have received from the Lord. Our oldest daughter was stricken with pneumonia. We had the doctor's advice which was to keep her in a warm room, and some medicine. The Lord completely healed her that night. Our son in law was stricken with hemorrhage at 1 o'clock in the morning. Prayers were made for him and he went to work as usual next day. Once, when I was taken with great pains in my side, my wife said we had better send for the doctor, 'Yes' I said, 'let us know what this is.' When the doctor arrived, he asked, 'What are the symptoms?' 'It's like someone driving a knife in my side.' I replied. 'Oh, pleurisy', said the doctor, 'send to the surgery.' But I got out of bed on to my knees and prayed, 'Dear Lord, the doctor says I have pleurisy, please heal me,' and got back bed, but never had another twitch. In 1914 I had a terrible bent knee develop which surprised the doctor and everyone that saw it. Many of my friends of the opinion I would never work again. But we committed the matter to the Lord and it began to reduce and in 3 weeks I was working again.

Our eldest boy was injured in the colliery soon after he started work. A lot of blood accumulated on the spinal column which caused paralysis and was taken to hospital for observation. Request for prayer was sent to Penygroes. The Lord heard and healed him. And the next x-rays showed no clot to the astonishment of doctors and nurses.

Idols

Just after my baptism in water the Holy Spirit began to deal with me about my 'idols'. First tobacco. My conscience being disturbed about it, so I thought I would reduce my use of it. I was using 6 oz a week, so I brought it down to 1 oz a week and thought I was doing very well. But still no peace. My pipe was before me all through service. Until one Sunday evening, the superintendent spoke on David killing Goliath. I remember his text. 'Go and the Lord be with you.' He referred to many idols, among them tobacco. That's me I said. And says he, 'you have got your idol down'. That's me I said. Now he said 'David didn't only get him down, but he ran, took his sword and cut his head off. Who is going to do that tonight?' And up went my hand. 'Thank God I would sooner that than have £5' he said. At this time, I had a gold chain which I used to think a great deal of. Being able to swank in the public houses over my companions. But my thoughts were not easy in God's house. So I sold the gold chain for £5 and gave the money to the Lord's work.

Restitution

There was an old gentleman that used to mend the trams on top of the colliery. In those days the tram was made of wood. And one night the old gentleman William Jordan had left his wood chisel on a tram. Myself and another young man made a run for this chisel and I won. I kept that chisel for some years but when the baptism of the Holy Spirit came, the thought also came to me about that chisel. But it was humiliating to have to take it back, but by God's grace I did it.

J. J. had tramped from Abertillery to Waunlwyd to find work, and had 3/9 worth of food from an old woman that was keeping a little shop in her house. 20 years went by, the Holy Spirit said, pay that 3/9 you owe. The old lady was dead, but J. J. sent 5/- to her husband who was still alive.

Another brother had stolen a hatchet from a fellow workman in the colliery where he was working and had sold it to a man in another colliery, the Holy Spirit said, 'Go and confess it and pay for it.'

Appendix A2

Ephraim Morris' Testimony (Written in 1973)

To write about what happened fifty years ago is a test of memory, and, without doubt, many events and persons involved will suffer from lack of appreciation and mention for the part they played in the birth of Bethel, and to all those quiet saints to whom credit is due, and on whom the glare of publicity never shone, I pay my respects and tribute.

Bethel was a visible sign that Beaufort had been blessed by a visitation from above, and many souls have seen the ladder of communication with heaven, and known ministrations of heavenly origin. Bethel, as a building, could never claim merit for its beauty or artistry, nor will it ever take its place among the great buildings of our land, yet, created from an almost derelict barn of a warehouse—disused and vacant—here, in this converted slum shambles, God, by his Holy Spirit dwelt, and it became the gateway to heaven for many precious souls. In this place, nobodies became notables: men and women of half a century ago, who were oppressed by poverty, living in conditions undreamed of today, having no hope in this life, and hitherto knowing nothing of the salvation that grace had provided. Fifty years ago we shared our bread. We shared our clothes. No man had two suits or pairs of shoes, and more often than not no overcoat, and fortunate to have a second shirt! Money was scarce; many were in debt because of low wages, strikes, and lockouts. This may sound exaggerated in this day and age, but the writer is one who lived through this era and experienced these difficulties. I am not writing these words to disparage these dear ones I knew, worked and lived with, knelt and prayed with, shared and sacrificed with. Oh no! My purpose is to magnify God's grace; the riches of his grace, who came to preach to the poor and set the captives free!

In this atmosphere, men were raised as firebrands, full of zeal, with practical experience of God and their Saviour. With no social standing, no umbrella of financial security, no pretensions to superiority, nothing in this world to claim and own, yet these men had the treasures of revelation and things divine, and who's preaching and power with God has not been surpassed.

The voice of God was heard in Bethel. There was a real reverence, and no one would dare to eat at the Lord's Table whose hands and heart were not clean. The evidence of the presence of the Lord was shown by the number of souls saved, in the expansion of the fellowship through the Monmouthshire valleys, in the growth of the church, but above all in the many, many trophies of grace who lived anew among their neighbours and companions as glowing testimonies. In the pits where we worked we sang and testified; day and night we preached the Lord Jesus Christ on street corners. We had no mechanical means of transport, but we walked mile after mile over hill and dale, carrying the vision that had become our purpose for living.

So to those in the district and area, who were not born in the those days, let me say to you that only eternity will spell out the effect, world-wide, that the events of fifty years ago engendered, and the grand folk who came out of the night of despair and degradation, to become self-sacrificing and noble in soul and spirit, thereby enriching family life and handing to their posterity a new way of living, a higher standard of attainment through the knowledge of Jesus Christ and his amazing love.

The names and labours of those at the helm of this movement have been spoken of often. I knew these men intimately, shared in their travail of soul, laboured throughout the valleys and was privileged to be counted in their number. I give thanks to God that I was counted worthy to suffer for his name's sake with them, but more so that it was mine to share in the joy of heaven when even one repentant sinner—and there were many, many such occasions—accepted Christ as their Saviour. I know assuredly that God is not in debt to any man, for he is lavish in giving in time and in eternity, and his rewards outweigh his demands. His strength and love span our feeble efforts, his purposes outlive our day and generation, and although almost all the heroes of fifty years ago have passed beyond the veil of time "HE REMAINETH."

May I be permitted to speak of the ministry of the preached word at Bethel. It was profound, rich in conception and presentation, born of sincerity, clothed with inspiration and preached with tongues of fire. We knew how to suffer trial and temptation; we knew poverty, too, and had nothing to glory in but Christ. Men who tumbled out of bed into the bowels of the earth to earn their daily bread, found the "Bread of Life" broken for them by the Spirit of God, and their eyes were opened to the secrets of their salvation.

What of prophetic ministry? Anyone who remembers those early days cannot forget the wonderful utterances, the heart-searching and personal words from the Lord. Jesus was in the midst, and we believed the prophets and accepted them as any other calling in the church. We progressed in spiritual gifts in variety, and the congregation was engulfed in worship and praise. Paul knew the value of spiritual gifts for he advised the early church to covet them, a very strong word meaning to "desire with intensity", and this was our aim at Bethel. We found it rewarding. They gave us something different from the normal way of worship, for a church without them has little or no appeal. What an asset and a testimony to have a spiritually gifted congregation, moved by the Holy Ghost! Those who despise spiritual gifts must be, unlike Paul, arrogant in self-sufficiency, labouring in vain, fishing in the night and catching nothing. What reward is there in an empty net or church?

A word must be spoken about the help and ministry afforded by the brethren from the assemblies in the Rhondda district, also from Hereford, and even more so from the leaders of the church in Penygroes. If the pulpit at Bethel could speak, it would utter names of saints and ministers now in glory, men of vision, of power and purpose, great men, men of oratory and a heavenly message. It would remind you of the zeal, the single-mindedness and the richness of revelation manifested by those who stood to minister. It would also speak of the congregation facing it, whose hunger for truth was so manifest; whose response was so spontaneous; whose "Amens" and "Alleluias" rang out and whose singing and praising rose in volume as the sound of many waters.

It would witness, too, to the many tears of repentance shed to the cries of "Lord have mercy on me!" and then to the joy displayed as chains fell off and prisoners were set free. Yes! The pulpit could speak of the sick in mind and body who came asking "Where is your great physician?" and, finding Him were restored to a new life and vitality. There was also heard, the groanings of the spirit in unselfish supplications for the welfare of the redeemed, for the needy and for the weak and tempest tossed. But, above all, it heard the voice of God! It vibrated to the sound of a rushing mighty wind, and was sanctified by the presence of the Holy Spirit, whose purpose was to magnify the Lord Jesus.

None of us can claim originality of authorship of our salvation, we are all in debt to the Lord Jesus, and we all build on his foundation. We also follow others who have laid their bodies on the altar as living sacrifices, and who built worthy of their calling. May it please the Christ, whose church will be his bride, to find people who care and fulfil the trust that God has put upon them in preparing the church for that great day, for we shall all have our building tested. May it be worthy of the foundation, worthy of commendation.

To all at Bethel, may I say that to you has been given a wonderful heritage, a history that has the hallmark of the divine, and like Simeon of old, Beaufort can say, "MINE EYES HAVE SEEN THY SALVATION." My prayer is that you will prosper in all things spiritual for there are riches that can be stored in heaven, "Where neither moth nor rust can corrupt." We all must leave this world and its treasures behind, so may you all be found with treasures in heaven.

Appendix A3

T. T. Seabourne's Testimony (written circa 1970)

About Easter 1918 Pastor Stephen Jeffreys held a Pentecostal mission at Zion Baptist Church, Brynmawr. Among those present were Jacob Purnell, Ephraim Morris, Jim Seaborne, Charles and David Noble. During these meetings, Jim Seaborne received the baptism of the Holy Spirit. His brother Tom, who was living at Tarfanaubach, near Tredegar, was staying with his father at Clydach, Breconshire. Jim went and told Tom what had happened, and later, meeting with the other brethren, Tom asked them if they would visit his home and hold a meeting there. This invitation was accepted, and at this meeting, although not baptised with the Spirit, Tom received an anointing, but his wife was baptised, and a young man who was also present was saved. He was Mrs. Seaborne's brother, Jim Meale, who later became a minister in a Pentecostal church.

Later, the brethren, together with a Mr. Charles Bennett, started to hold meetings at the home of Charles Noble, in Noble Square, Brynmawr. Pastor Hodges of Hereford visited them there, and although at that time not attached to the Apostolic Church, he set them in order in an assembly. Charles was appointed as overseer, Jacob as an evangelist and David as a deacon. Later they held meetings in the home of David, and during this time—in which they were paying tithes and God was speaking to them through the prophetic word—some problems arose, chiefly because some of the brethren wanted to obey the prophetic word. They decided to meet and talk things over, but because they could not agree, Jacob, Ephraim, Tom and Jim decided to leave the other brethren, and took their tithes with them.

It became necessary for these brethren to do something for themselves about meetings, so they decided to hold them in Tom's home in Tarfanaubach, which caused quite a stir and much persecution. They also held services in Sardis chapel in Beaufort (more familiarly known as "Jim John's" chapel), and at Jacob's home in Beaufort on Sunday evenings. Open-air meetings were also held, and at one of these early meetings in South Street, Beaufort, a man who had been drinking called them into his home, and before they left, in the early hours of the morning, he was gloriously saved. This was the first convert in Beaufort, Mr. W. Porter, fishmonger. His next-door neighbour, a Mr. Windsor Davies, had been saved previously and was attending the Wesleyan church, which he left to join with the brethren. He subsequently opened his home to allow meetings to be held there. During this period, Pastor and Mrs. Hodges visited Beaufort, and on one Sunday evening, at Jacob's house, Mrs. Hodges lectured on the Tabernacle.

Up to this time, no contact had been made with the Apostolic Church, although the brethren were aware that an Apostolic convention was to be held at Dowlais at Easter time. They went to this convention at which Pastors J. J. Williams and J. Forward were ministering, and had a conversation with brother Isaac Roberts, who was in charge of the convention. He advised them to contact Penygroes, which they subsequently did. At a later date, the brethren attended their first convention at Penygroes. Money was short, so they travelled on bicycles. As they were going down the steep hill between Merthyr and Hirwaun, the brakes of Jacob's bicycle failed. He called on the brethren to try to stop him, but they mistook his cries for shouts of "Hallelujah!" and replied in like terms. Miraculously, the Lord's hand was revealed and he came safely to a stop. No doubt, this was an attempt, on the part of the enemy, to foil the Divine Will in Jacob's life.

Jacob had heard that some of the brethren from Penygroes were going to hold meetings over a weekend at Abergavenny. Without their knowledge, he had bills printed that an Apostolic convention was to be held that same weekend at Beaufort. The brethren from Penygroes, Pastors D. P. Williams, Jones Williams and Omri Jones came by train to Beaufort on their way to Abergavenny. They got off the train and were informed of the convention that had been announced. They were perplexed, but the Lord gave the answer. They went to the old waiting room where Pastor Dan enquired of the Lord to direct them through the prophetic word. The direction, which God gave them, was for Pastors D. P. and Jones Williams to come to Beaufort on the Sunday, and Pastor Omri Jones to stay in Abergavenny. So the first Apostolic meeting in Beaufort was actually held in an old railway waiting room!

During this time, Jacob was given an old coachman's coat on condition that he would wear it. This coat began to be much talked about, so that many people came to see it, and God was using this coat to clothe many with the "garment of righteousness." They were much helped during this period by Pastor W. James who came to Beaufort and stayed for about three months. Brother Isaac Roberts from Dowlais also gave much help. Brother Roberts and others from Dowlais also assisted while meetings were held in Tarfanaubach, but these did not continue for long.

As time went on, the work settled to a more definite pattern. On Sundays, meetings were held at Beaufort Hill Primary School, on Mondays and Saturdays at Sardis chapel, and on Thursdays at the home of Mrs. Lloyd. This was an ex-army hut that had been erected after the first world war to help solve the housing problem. To all these places, people were coming and being saved, so much so that there was need for further establishing the assembly. This was done on 22nd July 1922; two years after Jacob had been set in charge of the work. Pastors Tom Rees and Omri Jones visited the district, during which time the Lord set apart brothers T. Seaborne and Phillip Williams to be elders. This was done in Sardis because as yet there was no Apostolic building in Beaufort.

For a long time, the brethren responsible had been anxious to acquire a place of their own in which to worship. They had been seeking since the time they left the Pentecostal church and enquiring whenever there seemed to be possibilities. It seemed that they were over-anxious, for at one time a prophetic word was given to them, and the Lord said, "You are too anxious to get a place of your own, but I have a place for you, and when you have a congregation, I will have a place ready for you to go into."

A little later, the brethren from Penygroes who were responsible for buildings visited Beaufort, and an old building which at an earlier period had been used as a stable, and later as a rag-stores, was purchased and renovated. On April 22nd 1923, Bethel was opened, with much rejoicing and thanks. On 27th April, 32 people were baptised in water, and a week later, a further number were also baptised. The first woman to be baptised was Mrs. T. Seaborne, and during this service, brothers Jim and Tom Seaborne were also baptised. This was the second time for them to be baptised, having previously gone through the waters of baptism without realising its significance. The opening of Bethel in April 1923 was a fulfilment of the prophecy before mentioned.

Appendix A4

Pastor Jacob Purnell's Testimony as printed in: 'Souvenir' Exhibiting the Movements of God in The Apostolic Church issued in Commemoration of the Opening of the Apostolic Temple, Penygroes, 1933.

2 Chronicles 20 v 20.

I shall not be able to state all the wonderful things, seen and heard, of the work in Monmouthshire. But it is with joy I can truly declare that the secret of the prosperity of such a work is due to the fact that the nature and principle of the truth in the text quoted has been our possession, namely: -

Faith in the unchangeable God.

Faith in the prophets and their message.

My early life and conversion.

It is necessary for me to record this, because of the link between Jacob and Bethel, the place of God's choice. Born of humble parentage, my parents being yet unsaved, yet the God of all grace visited our home during the 1904 revival and saved some of my family. I was then 13 years of age. My conversion at this time was remarkable in this sense. I was saved in the vestry of Zion Baptist Church, Brynmawr. I was sitting between the seats, rejoicing in the assurance of my salvation. Some wonderful power swept over my soul. The Bible became my meat and drink. This was at the age of 13, and I rejoiced in that blessing for many years. Sorry to state, a luke-warmness came over God' people, and also over my soul, so that I became a religious and luke-warm young man, and lost the sense of victory. Then I did what most young men do – I married, which caused me to move to a place called Beaufort.

Yes, a beautiful castle it is in more senses than one, due to sacred associations, namely the unveiling of God himself, and the raising of good, upright, holy characters from time to time. It was at this place that the mysterious call of God came to my soul. While attending Zoar Baptist Church, seated in the gallery between 8 o'clock and 9 o'clock in the evening, the voice of God came to my soul, calling for complete consecration. I yielded when the invitation was given, raised my hand as a sign, and then something wonderful happened in my life. My soul expanded, holy desires were born within me. I became a sincere, active worker in the church. In the midst of my activities, the call developed, and the voice within spoke louder and louder "LEAVE THIS PLACE!" I was in a struggle because of friendships forged and fellowship enjoyed. Eventually, I obeyed the voice, left the church I loved to do his will, certain of the fact that the Good Shepherd was guiding me. John 13 v 4 was the scripture given by the Spirit. As I followed the light, the darkness increased and eventually I found Matthew 10 vv 34–39 to be perfectly true in my own experience. It was at this point of testing that the good hand of God imparted to me the definite experience of sanctification and also the baptism of the Holy Spirit. Three months later, I spoke in an unknown tongue.

The Crisis

Jacob alone, no assembly to attend. Oh! How I longed for others to find what I had found. Now, like Elisha, who left the plough to follow his master, so I had the witness, that having obeyed the call, and being favoured with the blessing of the Spirit, it was a sign he desired others to enter into its enjoyment and power. While praying in secret, I was overwhelmed with the Spirit, speaking in other tongues, followed by interpretation – the audible voice of God. The burden of the message was "Stand thou alone, I will not fail thee, I will work." I assuredly gathered that the Lord desired me to stand in the open-air alone, and that he would work. The scene, the time, the witness given at that first time I stood I can never forget. I knew that as I stood alone from time to time, a glorious work was before me. In a while, I met two angels, yes, such they were to me, in the persons of brothers Thomas and James Seabourne. True as steel, they joined me in open-air work, and shortly after, another came along, Ephraim Morris, making four in all, the ranks were swelling. We decided to rent a meeting place, the name of which was "Sardis" (having a name that it liveth and is dead). But four living creatures entered; here we had great times in prevailing prayer. The Lord gave us encouragement in saving a notable religious sinner. Two other sisters were also saved, making the number to seven, two of the company walking five miles to the meeting place. Wonderful to relate, Sardis was the birthplace of the Apostolic vision in the Monmouthshire valleys. Here God revealed himself to us in the prophetic ministry in a wonderful way, and implanting faith in our hearts to believe it was his voice, we saw the vision of the plan of his church.

Hearing of a place called Penygroes, where God was speaking, we arranged to go to the Convention in August 1921. It is interesting to know how we got there but space will not permit me to relate. Here we entered into an enquiry regarding the Apostolic vision with the President of the Apostolic Church, the Apostle D. P. Williams. Having gathered that they were going to a place called Abergavenny, an evening was promised for Beaufort. But while returning home, I thought over the visit to Abergavenny, and only an evening promised to us. Jacob was at work, planning great things, and only seven in number! So we made our plans with big bills. This we can never forget, the bills and the posters headed thus:

RED LETTER DAY AUGUST 1921

APOSTOLIC CHURCH CONVENTION AT SARDIS CHURCH

(kindly lent)

AUGUST 27th over AUGUST 29th.

When I recall what a convention is, I smile! Yet I say, although at the time we were not Apostolic, the Lord was in it. On Saturday evening, I met the 6.10 train at Beaufort station. The two apostles and prophets were on their way to Abergavenny, and did not intend there to be at a convention in Beaufort. I can see them as I showed them the poster! They all came out onto the platform. Wonderful! Pastor D. P. prayed on the platform saying, "Lord, what shall we do?" The Lord spoke through the prophet Jones Williams saying, "The apostle who prayed and the channel should stay over the Sunday. The other apostle and the prophet are to come on Monday." We had a blessed time, I may state. The ministering of the servants was owned of God, and it was on the Sunday afternoon that we decided to submit to God's order and sweet will.

Apostolic Assembly Formed

Seven of us were received into fellowship. Afterwards, the Lord spoke through the prophet and I was called and anointed to be pastor and overseer of a flock of six on August 29th. The other apostle and prophet, J. O. Jones, came along according to the word of the Lord. In this meeting we had a blessed time and a few were sealed with the Holy Spirit.

Prophetical Era in my Experience

The Lord spoke through the prophet J. O. Jones saying: "I will use thee; I will bless thee; I will cause my word to flow from here and every valley shall hear of my doings."

In August 1921, we were told by the Lord to apply for the use of the local primary school in which to hold our services on Sundays. This we did, and we obtained the use of the smallest room for three services. The room seated about 30. It was more like a sideshow than anything else. Sanballat's followers came, they ridiculed, rushing in and out, but we were unaffected. We prayed on and praised God! The room became over-crowded, so we looked for the best and largest room seating 200 to 300, which was packed each evening. Surely, the church here was born in Apostolic fashion! Every night we held cottage meetings, our homes were the Lord's; every room was occupied by the crowds who came. We took the spoiling of our goods joyfully. God was working and saving. Tippet players, boxers, skittlers, and cardsharps were swept into the kingdom. Drunkards and swearers were saved, among them a trophy of grace, Phillip Williams, known to many. We saw incurable cures. We still have on record miraculous cases of healing from dumbness, consumption, cripples, and other incurable diseases. God baptised many in His Spirit, enabling them to speak in other tongues and prophesy, without the touch of human hands. Prophetic channels were born in revival power. Much persecution followed. Our membership reached 80 in a short time. We recognised the fulfilment of the Prophetic Word. I should state here, that Pastor W. James, known to all in Monmouthshire at that time, was a means in God's hands of holding and strengthening us in the Apostolic faith, having had greater experience. He spent months with us, labouring and toiling as a shepherd. This is fresh in our memory with God.

Does God Speak Through His Prophets Today?

During a visit of Pastor W. J. Williams in September 1921, the Lord spoke, saying that he would grant us a stone building, which would be a Bethel indeed. Now this was wonderful, as the cost of materials was very high at that time, and obtaining a stone building was seemingly impossible. BUT HE WHO PROMISED WAS WELL ABLE.

Opening of New Church 1923

The opening meetings at "Bethel", Beaufort, were held from April 5th over April 22nd. This was a witness to all that this work was to be a lasting one. Fifty were baptised in water at the opening of the new hall. Progress was remarkable. In August 1921, we were seven in number. April 1923 found us with 80 in membership, and a lovely church in which to worship. In April 1923, a remarkable prophecy came through Pastor J. O. Jones. "Jacob and Bethel are mine, saith the Lord. This is the place of my choice. Rivers will flow from here; every village and town will I touch, even to Newport. I will even send some of you to cities."

This was a great demand on our faith. We believed, we cried to God, we set to work. The work spread like wild fire through the valleys. Doors were opening. Each step we took was on the prophetic word. Oh! How we proved its value, choosing, preserving, establishing; no tongue can tell. I make my confession: I am, and have been, blessed of God, used of God and won favour due to the power of the spoken Word towards me. Its value is untold. "HE SPAKE AND IT WAS DONE, HE COMMANDED AND IT STOOD FAST" The prophet, Omri Jones has spent much time in Monmouthshire these eleven years. Prophecies uttered in relation to persons, places, details etc. have truly been fulfilled.

Experience is Indubitable

We have proved beyond all doubt, through set prophetic channels, that our God is a God to be enquired of. There are opposing forces of unbelief against the spoken word. But we have irrefutable proof of its reality in the lives of members in the assemblies in Monmouthshire.

The Newport Churches

The Newport churches are a fulfilment of prophecy uttered in Bethel in April 1923. It is very wonderful that the farewell meeting was held at Beaufort on the anniversary of the opening of Bethel, and also the induction service was held in Newport in April 1932, the prophecy finding its fulfilment in a person, place and month, 9 years later. In 1923, Newport was promised in prophecy. In September 1931, a prophecy came forth in Bethel, Beaufort, saying "It is time for you to possess the land and I have promised that many of my servants shall minister in Newport in the near future." I found myself in Newport in April 1932. We have made great progress in twelve months. We have 3 assemblies established and are still advancing. "THIS IS THE LORD'S DOING AND IT IS MARVELLOUS IN OUR EYES."

Summary of Movements

In 1918 I was alone in the blessing in Beaufort.

In 1921 the Apostolic Church was formed in Beaufort. 6 members and 1 overseer.

In 1933 there were 20 churches established, over 100 members, 1 apostle and 1 pastor in full time ministerial work.

In 1921, the first convention in Beaufort had 20 in number. At the present convention (1933), the largest church in Beaufort is filled, continually seating 900.

At the first watch-night service, 30 attended. Now about 1,000 present themselves.

Beaufort Church Membership c. 1930

Appendix A5

Brief Recollections by Harry Evans (written 2015)

My first recollection of the Apostolic Church is when I was seven or eight years old.

Prior to attending the Apostolic Church, we regularly attended Libanus Presbyterian Church in Worcester Street, Brynmawr.

My early recollections of the Apostolic Church are from when it was over the Indian and China tea shop in Beaufort Street. I cannot remember who the overseer was at the time, but I am told that it was a man by the name of Charlie Bennet. I can remember Charlie Bennet. He had two daughters who were my senior by many years; their names were Maisie and Violet.

The meetings took place in what was then called the 'upper room'. It was quite well attended, as I remember. I can also bring to memory two men that came from Ebbw Vale, namely, Roy Galloway and David John Edwards. They would both play their violins. Although I was quite young, the services on a Sunday morning were quite interesting. When the opportunity was given for reading of the Psalms and testimonies, folk were more than eager to stand up to give their experience of what God had done throughout the week. Many a time it would be said that by the middle of the week, mothers had no food to put on the table for the children when they came home at midday for their lunch. Things were much different from today. Children today have their meals provided in the schools. Mothers would relate how they prayed, and by the time that lunchtime came (by various means), God supplied their need.

Although quite young, one could feel that the atmosphere in the room was absolutely charged with the power and presence of God. Of course, Pastor Jacob Purnell was then the district Pastor.

My mother was the organist at that time.

As time went by, I got to know and remember the names of quite a number who attended. Two of the older ladies were known as Nanny Bailey and Mrs. Ford. Mrs. Ford was quite elderly, and the mother of Mr. Tom Ford, who became a pastor and missionary to West Africa. Nanny Bailey lived a short distance away from the hall, but Mrs. Ford lived in Winchestown, and had to walk two or three miles to the church. Very few had cars at that time. The daughter of Mrs. Ford, and the sister of Tom Ford was named Jane Ann Ford. She had a number of children. Amongst the eldest was Lilian. Lilian would bring with her two younger sisters, and an older brother, whose name was Selwyn. My recollections are of them attending Sunday School. You can imagine, walking that distance from Winchestown on a wet day, they would be soaked to the skin.

The upper room, I would say, was not the most convenient or best of places. We had to climb a flight of stairs, and pass a door on the left which was always open. There was often a roaring fire in the room, and a man who was not very pleasant and kind. But it could be said, although I was young, the meetings from the experience that I have gained to this moment of time, were very powerful. God was moving in a wonderful and powerful way.

We were pleased to learn that a new church was to be built in Clydach Street. The builder was known as Dai Miles. He had a son by the name of Wilf Miles who, as I remember, joined the church when it opened in 1939.

I can relate many of the Overseers and Elders. At that time there were quite a number of Elders. My father was an Elder, George Parfitt was both an Elder and Sunday School Superintendent. Richard Purnell (Jacob's brother), Joe Prosser, Tom Davies, Charlie Bennet, Tom Withers, George Woolridge, Billy Kedward, David Phipps. Martin Hill, also an Elder, had a wonderful conversion. He was, like many in those days, a drunkard. After the drink he felt that he could fight anyone, including the police. God did a wonderful work in his life, and when the Heads of the Valley road opened from Brynmawr to Abergavenny, he was waiting with his bicycle, to make the first ride down the new road. If my memory serves me right, he was almost 90 years of age then, and he was allowed to travel the new road before any traffic was allowed down. Some of the Overseers were Albert George Bull, Ted Evans (father of Collin Evans), and David John Pratten.

Pastor Purnell then lived in King Street, Brynmawr, and when he was not attending other churches in the District, he would be present in Brynmawr. The name given to that Assembly was Moriah. Richard Purnell had a son who also became a pastor, namely George Purnell, who later went on to serve the Lord in our Canada churches. His wife's name was Laura.

In those days, the women sat on the right hand side of the church, and the men sat on the left. In Moriah, the organist was Miss Lilian Walters, whose very close friend was Miss Collins.

(Because of the good number of Eldership, many were sent to various Assemblies in the district, some as far as Llanhilleth. Some walked, and some travelled on bicycles.)

At some time in the experience of the Brynmawr Assembly, a band was formed. I can remember very well the bandmaster was a man by the name of Mr. George Webb who was formerly the bandmaster for the Salvation Army band. Both I and my brother Hedley played an instrument in the band. Hedley became a very proficient player of the trombone. Others, I recall, that played instruments in the band are: Albert Seabourne – cornet; Mr. George Woolridge – double bass; Tom Ford – trombone; Mr. Ben Evans (my father) – big drum. Also quite a number of others.

On one occasion we went to play at Rassau. My father asked Mr. Webb as to how to start marching. My father said, "I only know the military start off." Mr. Webb said that will be alright then. As soon as the big drum sounded, children and dogs came from everywhere to see what was going on!

Bibliography

Adams, K. & E. Jones. *A Pictorial History of Revival: The Outbreak of the 1904 Welsh Awakening.* Farnham: CWR, 2004.

Allen, David. *The Unfailing Stream, A Charismatic Church History in Outline.* Tonbridge: Sovereign World, 1994.

Apostolic Church. *Souvenir: Exhibiting the Movements of God in The Apostolic Church.* Llanelli: Mercury, 1933.

Barrat, T. B. *In the Days of the Latter Rain.* London: Elim Publishing Co., 1909. 2nd Edition, 1928.

Evans, Eifion. *Revival Comes to Wales, The Story of the 1859 Revival in Wales.* Bridgend: Evangelical Press of Wales 1959; 3rd Edition, 1986.

Evans, Eifion. *The Welsh Revival of 1904.* London: Evangelical Press, 1969; 2nd Edition, 1974.

Gee, Donald. *The Pentecostal Movement: A Short History and an Interpretation for British Readers.* Ebook: Read Books Ltd, 2013.

Gray-Jones, Arthur. *A History of Ebbw Vale.* Rogerstone: Gwent County Council 1970; 2nd Edition, 1992.

Hession, Roy. *We Would See Jesus.* Wendover: Rickfords 1958; Reprint, 2008.

Hunter, H. D. and C. M. Robeck Jnr. *The Asuza Street Revival and Its Legacy.* Eugene, OR: Wipf and Stock 2006; 2nd Edition, 2009.

Lowe, Karen. *Carriers of the Fire, The Women of the Welsh Revival 1904/05.* Llanelli: Shedhead Productions, 2004.

Palmer, Chris. *The Emergence of Pentecostalism in Wales.* London: Apostolos, 2016.

Parkinson, Roger. *Encyclopaedia of Modern Warfare.* London: Routledge & Kegan Paul, 1977.

Parrinder, Geoffrey. *A Concise Encyclopaedia of Christianity.* Oxford: One World, 1998.

Penn-Lewis, Jessie and Evan Roberts. *War on the Saints.* Full text unabridged edition. Kent: Diasozo Trust, 1973; 9th Edition, 1987.

Shaw, S. B. *The Great Revival in Wales.* Pensecola FL: Christian Life Books, 2002.

Thomas, Keith. Faces and Places of Ebbw Vale. Kerin, 1987.

Turnbull, T. N. *What God Hath Wrought.* Bradford: Puritan Press, 1959.

Turnbull, T. N. *Brothers in Arms.* Bradford: Puritan Press, 1963.

Weeks, Gordon. *Chapter Thirty-Two.* Barnsley: Gordon Weeks 2003.

Williams, D. *From a Gramp to his Great Grandson: A Grandfathers Testimony.* Tredegar, Paul Beynon, 1997.

Williams, D. P. *The Work of an Evangelist, his Calling, Qualifications and Equipment.* Llanelly, Apostolic Church, circa 1928.

Williams, D. P. *The Prophetical Ministry (or the Voice Gifts) in the Church.* Llanelly, Apostolic Church, 1931.

Williams, D. P. *Cradle of Mystery.* Edited by P. K. Yeoman. Swansea: Kingdom First Publishing, 2006.

Williams, Philip, J. *The Touch of the Masters Hand*. Bradford: Puritan Press, 1954.

Worsfold, James E. *The Origins of the Apostolic Church in Great Britain with a Breviate of its Early Missionary Endeavours*. Wellington: Julian Literature Trust, 1991.

Magazine Articles and Papers

Anderson, Allen. "To All Points of the Compass: The Azusa Street Revival and Global Pentecostalism." *AoG, Enrichment Journal* <http://enrichmentjournal.ag.org/200602> [2016].

Bradshaw, Robert. "Bending the Church to Save the World: The Welsh Revival of 1904." <http://theologicalstudies.org.uk> [1995].

Davies, Price. "The Beginning of the Pentecostal Movement in the Merthyr Borough". <www.dustandashes.com> [c. 1960].

Evans, E. G. "Monmouthshire Memories, A Brief Account of the Inception of the Apostolic Church in the Monmouthshire Valleys." *Apostolic Herald*, January, February & March 1972.

Gillan, Alexander, P. A. "History of the Holiness Movement in Great Britain." http://www.regal- network.com/chm/files/pdf/british_holiness_movement.pdf [1995] Rev. 2004.

Hayward, John. "Timeline of the Background to 1904–5 Welsh Revival." [2004] <www.churchmodel.org.uk>.

Kay, W. K. "Sunderland's Legacy in New Denominations" *JEPTA* 28(2) 2008, 183–199.

Pike, David Edward. "1849 Revival: Fruit in the Heads of the Valleys" <www.daibach-welldigger.blogspot.co.uk> October 2012.

Riches of Grace Vol. 2 No. 2 (July 1922).

Websites

Apostolic Church <http://apostolic-church.org/about-us/history>.

A Welsh Coal Mines Page <www.welshcoalmines.co.uk/Gwent/Wyllie.htm>.

British Religion in Numbers <http://www.brin.ac.uk/2011/uk-church-statistics-2005-15>.

Confidence <http://pentecostalarchives.org>.

Cwm Community Care <http://www.cwmcommunitycare.org.uk/waunlwyd-victoria-collierie/4558107657>.

Davies, Gwyn. The 1859 Revival – from a talk given at Heath Church, Cardiff <www.heath-church.org 2009>.

Parliament <http://www.parliament.uk/about/living-heritage/transformingsociety>.

Salvation Army <www.salvationarmy.org.uk/history>.

Smith Wigglesworth <www.smithwigglesworth.com>.

The Apostolic Faith <www.apostolicfaith.org/Library/Index/AzusaPapers.aspx>.

Welsh Newspapers <http://newspapers.library.wales/>.

BV - #0044 - 080526 - C0 - 216/138/7 - PB - 9781910942604 - Matt Lamination